Howls & Growls

FRENCH POEMS TO BARK BY

Howls & Growls

FRENCH POEMS TO BARK BY

English Translations by Norman R. Shapiro

Illustrations by Olga Pastuchiv

BLACK WIDOW PRESS

BOSTON

Publication of this book has also been aided by a grant from the Thomas and Catharine McMahon Fund of Wesleyan University, established through the generosity of the late Joseph McMahon.

Joseph S. Phillips and Susan J. Wood, Ph.D., Publishers
www.blackwidowpress.com

Illustrations and Art Direction: Olga K. Pastuchiv
Design, Typesetting & Production: Kerrie Kemperman

ISBN-13: 978-1-7338924-0-7

Printed in the United States

10 9 8 7 6 5 4 3 2 1

for Sean,
with thanks for his patience

Table of Contents

Preface by Norman R. Shapiro ~ 11

MARIE DE FRANCE (*ca.* 1160–*ca.* 1210)
  Of the Hound and a Ewe / *Dou chien e d'une berbis* ~ 15

EUSTACHE DESCHAMPS (*ca.* 1346–*ca.* 1406)
  A Peasant and His Hound / *D'un paisant et de son chien* ~ 19

JOACHIM DU BELLAY (*ca.* 1522–1560)
  Epitaph for a Dog / *Epitaphe d'un chien* ~ 23

ANTOINE FURETIÈRE (1619–1688)
  Many a Hound / *De plusieurs chiens* ~ 25

JEAN DE LA FONTAINE (1621–1695)
  The Dog Who Drops His Prey for Its Reflection /
  Le chien qui lâche sa proie pour l'ombre ~ 27
  The Dog Who Had His Ears Cut Short /
  Le chien a qui on a coupé les oreilles ~ 29

CHARLES PERRAULT (1628–1703)
  The Dog, the Cock, and the Fox /
  Le chien, le coq et le renard ~ 31

JEAN-BAPTISTE-JOSEPH WILLART DE GRÉCOURT
  (1684–1743)
  The Gascon Dog / *Le chien Gascon* ~ 33
  The Little Pup / *Le petit chien* ~ 35

NICOLAS GROZELIER (1692–1778)
  The Hound Who Bays at the Moon /
  Le chien qui aboie a la lune ~ 37
  The Farmer and His Four Dogs /
  Le fermier et ses quatre chiens ~ 39

CHRISTIAN GELLERT (1715–1769)
  The Faithful Hound / *Le chien fidèle* ~ 43

PRINCE IGNACY KRASICKI (1735–1801)
    The Two Dogs / *Les deux chiens* ~ 45
    The Hound and the Hunter/ *Le chien et le chasseur* ~ 47

JEAN-JACQUES-FRANÇOIS-MARIN BOISARD (1744–1833)
    The Buddhist Monk and the Hound / *Le bonze et le chien* ~ 49

ANTOINE VITALLIS (1749–1830)
    The Little Dog / *Le petit chien* ~ 51

JEAN-PIERRE CLARIS DE FLORIAN (1755–1794)
    The Guilty Hound / *Le chien coupable* ~ 55
    The Ewe and the Dog / *La brebis et le chien* ~ 61

ADELINE JOLIVEAU DE SEGRAIS (1756–1830)
    A Lesson Too Late / *L'éducation tardive* ~ 63
    The Cruel Hound / *Le mauvais chien* ~ 65

ANTOINE-VINCENT ARNAULT (1766–1834)
    The Dog and the Fleas / *Le chien et les puces* ~ 67

MARC-LOUIS DE TARDY (1769–1857)
    The Dog and the Cat / *Le chien et le chat* ~ 69

NAPOLÉON BONAPARTE (1769–1821)
    The Hound, the Rabbit, and the Hunter /
    Le chien, le lapin et le chasseur ~ 71

JEAN-JOSEPH-MARIUS DIOULOUFET (1771–1840)
    The Tiger and the Dog / *Lou tigre et lou chin* ~ 75

ABBÉ A.-L. GUILLOUTET (????–18??)
    The Old Mastiff / *Le vieux mâtin* ~ 77

GOSWIN-JOSEPH-AUGUSTIN DE STASSART (1780–1854)
    The Dog-Merchant / *Le marchand des chiens* ~ 79
    The Children, the Spaniel, and the Bulldog / *Les enfants,*
    l'épagneul et le bouledogue ~ 83

J.-J. ILDEPHONSE GUIEU (18??–18??)
  The Guilty Dog / *Le chien coupable* ~ 85
  Do and the Sick Dog / *Do et le chien malade* ~ 87

CLAUDE-THÉOPHILE DUCHAPT (1802–1858)
  The Hound Who Bays at the Moon /
  Le chien qui jappe après la lune ~ 89

VICTOR HUGO (1802–1885)
  Death of a Dog / *La mort d'un chien* ~ 91

PIERRE LACHAMBEAUDIE (1806–1872)
  The Chicken, the Fox, and the Hound /
  Le poulet, le renard et le chien ~ 93
  The Dog and the Lion / *Le chien et le lion* ~ 95

AUGUSTE FISCH (1814–1881)
  A Poodle's Revenge / *La vengeance d'un caniche* ~ 97

CHARLES BAUDELAIRE (1821–1867)
  The Dog and the Perfume Vial / *Le chien et le flacon* ~ 99

ANATOLE DE SÉGUR (1823–1902)
  The Sick Dog / *Le chien malade* ~ 101

VALÉRY DERBIGNY (mid-19th Century)
  The Hounds' Quarrel / *La querelle des chiens* ~ 105

EMILE COUTEAU (1837–1931)
  The Automobile / *L'Automobile* ~ 107

ANDRÉ GILL (1840–1885) and
  LOUIS DE GRAMONT (1854–1912),
  The Little Greyhound Bitch and the Urchin /
  La levrette et le gamin ~ 111

A. DE BLANCHE (????–????),
  The Dog One Would Drown / *Le chien qu'on noie* ~ 117

MAURICE ROLLINAT (1846–1903)
  The Mad Dog / *Le chien enragé* ~ 119
  Pistolet's Death / *Mort de pistolet* ~ 121

HENRY MACQUERON (1853 –1937)
  The Virtuous Dog / *Le chien vertueux* ~ 123
  The Dog and the Kitten / *Le chien et le petit chat* ~ 127
  The Dog and the Ass / *Le chien et le baudet* ~ 129

FRANCIS PICABIA (1879–1953)
  Ahead and Behind / *Entr'acte de cinq minutes* ~ 131

ABEL BONNARD (1883–1968)
  The Old Dog / *Le vieux chien* ~ 135

JULES SUPERVIELLE (1884–1960)
  The First Dog / *Le premier chien* ~ 137

PIERRE MENANTEAU (1895–1992)
  The Old Man and His Dog / *Le vieux et son chien* ~ 139

MAURICE CARÈME (1899–1978)
  The Little Dog / *Le petit chien* ~ 141
  The Child and The Dog / *L'enfant et le chien* ~ 143

JEAN FOLLAIN (1903–1971)
  The Schoolboys' Dog / *Le chien des écoliers* ~ 145

RAYMOND QUENEAU (1903–1976)
  "You've got to signal the driver…" /
  Il faut faire signe au machiniste ~ 147
  In Space / *Dans l'espace* ~ 149

[EUGÈNE] GUILLEVIC (1907–1997)
  The Little Pup / *Fabliette du petit chien* ~ 151

JEAN ANOUILH (1910–1987)
  The Couple and the Little Dog / *Le couple et le petit chien* ~ 153
  The Funeral / *L'enterrement* ~ 157

CARMEN BERNOS DE GASZTOLD (1919–1995)
  The Dog's Prayer / *Prière du chien* ~ 161

RENÉ-GUY CADOU (1920–1951)
  Of Horses and Dogs / *Des chevaux et des chiens* ~ 163

MADELEINE REYNAUD (contemp.)
  The Little Dog / *Le petit chien* ~ 165

KHAMLIÈNE NHOUYVANISVONG (contemp.)
  A Dog's Life / *Vie de chien* ~ 169

CHANTAL ABRAHAM (contemp.)
  My Friend My Chum / *Mon copain* ~ 171

PIERRE CORAN (pseud.) (b. 1934)
  The Greyhound and the Gazelle / *Le lévrier et la gazelle* ~ 175
  The Dogs and the European Parliament /
  Les chiens et le Parlement ~ 177
  The Dogs and the Saint-Bernard /
  Les chiens et le Saint-Bernard ~ 181
  The Tycoon and the Dogs / *Le magnat et les chiens* ~ 185

GÉRARD LE GOUIC (b. 1936)
  "When my dog looks at me…" /
  « *Quand ma chienne me regarde* » ~ 187

JEAN-PIERRE ANDREVON (b. 1937),
  Mummykins and Her Doggum-Woggums /
  Chien-chien à sa mémère ~ 189

MARC ALYN (pseud.) (b. 1937)
  Shadow Dog of Night / *Chien d'ombre dans la nuit* ~ 191

ROBERT PAQUIN (b. 1946)
  Found Again / *Retrouvé* ~ 195

JACQUES GOURVENNEC (1955–2013)
  "And my wife, and the roses, and the dog…" /
  « *Et ma femme et les roses et le chien…* » ~ 197

DANIEL BOY (contemp.)
  The Old Man and the Dog / *Le vieil homme et le chien* ~ 201

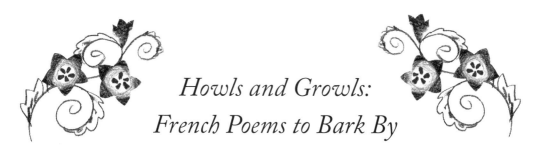

Howls and Growls: French Poems to Bark By

PREFACE

Much has been written about the comparative psychology of the "dog person" versus the "cat person." Not a psychologist myself, I am happy to admit that I am both. I am also a literary translator, devoted especially to French poetry.

It was not unusual, therefore, that several years ago I should decide to turn my talents in one—and eventually both—of their directions. Seeming to recall a proverb stating that the French love the dog but worship the cat, or something to that effect, I decided to turn first to the latter. The happy result was *Fe-Lines: French Cat Poems Through the Ages* (Illinois, 2015), elegantly illustrated by Olga Pastuchiv, and my literary cats have been meowing and purring through its pages since its appearance. So energetically, in fact, that I have frequently been asked by hopeful cat fanciers when I might be contemplating a second volume. To which I reply today with the second of the present two collections, compiled from poems that, originally intended to find a place in *Fe-Lines,* had had to be deleted for lack of space, and that now present themselves as: *Cats Great and Small, Cats All*—under the auspices of Black Widow Press, an elite publisher devoted to the art and craft of literary translation. Rather more reader-friendly than *Fe-Lines,* with originals and translations conveniently side-by-side, it still spans the centuries, offering well-known and lesser-known poets, and again enlivened by engaging illustrations.

Meanwhile the dogs have been lurking patiently in the wings. Some whimpering, some growling, some barking up their appropriate trees, and all ready to embark on their poetic ventures. Dogs of every variety; and a variety far greater than that among their feline cousins. Indeed, when I look at my own four cats—a Calico domestic shorthair, two Russian Blue, and a majestic Maine Coon—it is perfectly clear even to a non-scientist like myself, that, minor variations notwithstanding, they and others of their ilk are related to the Great Cats of the wild. When I look at my dog, on the other hand—a Shih-tsu puppy, mixed Maltese and Pekingese standing a scant ten inches off the ground—and visualize him between a Chihuahua on one side and a Great Dane on the other, it is only a supreme act of faith that can convince me that he, like all canines, is a *bona fide* descendant of the wolf.

Varieties of temperament as well, as readers will appreciate. And it is with reverence for this diversity of theirs, that Nature in her wondrous artistry has mysteriously bestowed on them, that I present these bilingual examples by French poets of nine-plus centuries, reflecting both chronological and formal variety, from several countries in addition to France, adding to those of a well-deserved celebrity—not only literary (*e.g.* even Napoléon Bonaparte!)—others scarcely known at all to the world of letters, and whom I am pleased to have rescued at least briefly from obscurity.

The poems in these two new collections—*Howls and Growls: French Poems to Bark By* and its companion volume, *Cats Great and Small: Cats All*—might easily have been multiplied many fold—a tribute to the literary popularity of the Dog—especially in the rich verse-fable genre*—and to the Cat as well, the big and the little, from the swift and sleek Great Cat predators to the lovably sly and frisky household companions. May they enjoy the same admiration as their predecessors, and may their readers enjoy the jungle roars, the meows and the mews of their feline muse no less.

—*Norman R. Shapiro*

---

* See Jean-Claude Hermans, *Le Chien dans les Fables* (Paris, Société des Ecrivains, 2011).

MARIE DE FRANCE *(ca. 1160–ca. 1210)*

Dou chien e d'une berbis

Or cunte d'un Chien mentéour
De meintes guises trichéour,
Qui une Berbis emplèda
Devant Justise l'amena.
Se li ad un Pain démandei
K'il li aveit, ce dist, prestei ;
La Berbiz tut le dénoia
E dit que nus ne li presta.
Li Juges au Kien demanda
Se li de ce nus tesmoins a
Il li respunt k'il en ad deus,
C'est li Escufles è li Leus.
Cist furent avant amenei,
Par sèrement unt afermei
Ke ce fu voirs que li Chiens dist :
Savez pur-coi chascuns le fist,
Que il en atendoient partie
Se la Berbis perdeit la vie.
Li Jugièrres dunc demanda
A la Berbis k'il apela,
Pur coi out le Pain renoié
Ke li Chienz li aveit baillié,
Menti aveit pur poi de pris
Or li rendist ainz qu'il fust pis.
La Chative n'en pot dune rendre
Se li convint sa leine vendre,
Ivers esteit, de froit fu morte,

14

MARIE DE FRANCE *(ca. 1160–ca. 1210)*

Of the Hound and a Ewe

The tale is told about a hound
Who many a strategy had found
To lie and cheat: what I aver
Is proven in these lines. The cur
Had brought a ewe before the court,
Avowing, in a false report,
That she owed him a loaf of bread,
For he had lent her one, he said,
And now he wanted it returned.
The ewe, quite innocent, had spurned
The dog's request, telling the oaf
That never had she had a loaf
To lend! Whereat the judge approached
The plaintiff-hound, and duly broached
A question of the law. To wit:
"That loan… Did others witness it?"
"Indeed! The wolf and kite," replied
The dog, claiming the pair espied
The whole affair. At which, the two
Come, summoned. "What he says is true,"
Said pair affirms, unflinchingly,
Certain that, if the beast should be
Put to death, neither would demur
But would feast on the whole of her!
Verdict? The judge reproached our poor
Ewe, deep in dour discomfiture:
"Guilty, madame! For shame! Now, give

Li Chiens vient, sa part enporte
È li Escoffles d'autre par ;
E puis li Leus, cui trop fu tard
Ke la char entre aus detreite
Car de viande aveient sofreite.
È la Berbiz plus ne vesqui
E ses Sires le tout perdi.

MORALITÉ

Cest essample vus voil mustrer,
De meins Humes le puis pruver
Ki par mentir è par trichier,
Funt les Povres suvent plédier.
Faus tesmoignages avant traient,
De l'avoir as Povres les paeint ;
Ne leur chaut que li Las deviengne,
Mais que chascuns sa part en tiengne.

Monsieur his loaf, if you would live!"
Breadless, the drear defendant had
Little to do, in wool well-clad,
But sell her wool to buy a bread
And give the hound that one instead.
Which she did... Winter's cold soon chilled her—
Fresh-shorn and bare—and promptly killed her!
Tasty sheep flesh being all too rare,
The hound and kite wolfed down their share.
For the wolf? Nothing! Ewe adieu...
(And for the shepherd? One less ewe!)

MORAL

By this moral exemplum, I
Would show how often men who lie
And cheat, give many a pauper cause
To bear the burden of the Law's
Improper wiles: perjurers will
Ransack the poor and do them ill.
It matters not the wrack and woe
Wrought on the weak and weary! No!
Churls' evil weighs nor whit nor jot
If theirs the benefit begot!

EUSTACHE DESCHAMPS *(ca. 1346–1406)*

D'un paisant et de son chien

Un paisant avoit un chien
De grant exploit, jeune et puissant,
Fort et hardi, si l'ama bien,
Car toute beste fut prenant,
Et si gardoit diligemment
Son hostel de jour et de nuit ;
Manger lui fist de maint deduit,
Et des loups son tropiau garda.
Or devint vieulx; lors le destruit :
Quant fruit fault, desserte s'en va.

Son vivre en son aage ancien
Lui restraint et le va foulant
Pour en chaiel qui ne vault rien,
Dont le viel chien est moult dolent
Et dit : « J'ay perdu mon jouvent,
Qui cuidoie cueillir le fruit
De mon jeune temps; or suy vuit
D'avoir guerdon. Advisez la ;
Notez bien ce proverbe tuit:
'Quant fruit fault, desserte s'en va.' »

Bien voy ceste figure et tien;
Reduire la puis proprement
A mon service, et pour ce vien
A conclure semblablement:
Quant j'ay servi treslonguement,

EUSTACHE DESCHAMPS *(ca. 1346–ca. 1406)*

A Peasant and His Hound

A peasant had a hound: young, bold,
Victor against his every prey.
Fearless protector of the fold,
Staunch sentinel—by night, by day—
He kept the fearsome wolf at bay,
Guarding the household, snug abed.
Loved by his master. he was fed
Naught but the finest fare… But he
Grows old, and he ought well be dead:
When fled the fruit, farewell the tree.

Where now those meats and sweets untold?
Where now the love, the work, the play?
A callow pup has been enrolled
To take his place; mere worthless stray!
Laments the hound, in disarray:
"My youth, with all its pleasures? Fled!
Now, none but hollow days ahead…
Look at my plight and chastened be!
How true the saying, most often said:
'When fled the fruit, farewell the tree!'"

I see this fiction and behold
The hound's dejection with dismay:
Undone, unwanted, unconsoled…
That peasant and his hound portray
My plight as well. Ah, welladay!

Lors vient ingratitude et bruit;
D'estat me despointe et me nuit.
Las! ma viellesce que fera?
Bien puis dire com vray instruit:
« Quant fruit fault, desserte s'en va. »

L'ENVOY

Prince, faictes faire autrement
A ceuls qui servent loyaument,
Vostre regne mieulx en vauldra;
Ne faictes com le paisant
Fist a son chien mauvaisement.
Quant fruit fault, desserte s'en va.

Cast out, scorn heaped upon my head…
Ah, age! What sport you make of me!
And so I sigh, dispirited:
"When fled the fruit, farewell the tree."

ENVOY

Prince, let not faithful liege, I pray,
Be cast so carelessly away,
Like hound, though fine his pedigree.
Pay loyalty its due; thus may
Your reign be praised, and none may say:
"When fled the fruit, farewell the tree."

JOACHIM DU BELLAY *(ca. 1522–1560)*

Epitaphe d'un chien

Ce bon Hurauld, qui souloit estre
Le mignon de Jacquet son maistre,
Hurauld venu du bas Poitou
Sur les doulces rives d'Anjou,
Pour garder le troppeau champestre:

Pendant que la bande compaigne
Des autres chiens, sur la campaigne
Dormant gisoit deça, dela,
Faisant le guet sur ce bord là,
Ou Meine à Loyre s'accompaigne:

Ce bon chien sur tous chiens fidele
Defendit de la dent cruelle
Les aignelets, mais ce pendant
Il mourut en les defendant,
Digne de louange immortelle.

JOACHIM DU BELLAY *(ca. 1522–1560)*

Epitaph For A Dog

Hurault, that good and stalwart hound,
Jacquet's most cherished pet, who found
His way to these climes Angevin
From Bas Poitou, and who, herein,
Guarded the flocks the country round…

None of his fellow dogs would deign—
Lying about our fair terrain—
Remain awake, but slept and slept
Whilst he his watchful vigil kept,
Here, where the Loire meets with the Maine.

Faithful was he, ever defending
Lambkins from certain death impending,
Under the vicious fang, and hence,
Perished one day in their defense,
Worthy of grateful praise unending.

ANTOINE FURETIÈRE *(1619–1688)*

De plusieurs chiens

> Dans la cuisine d'un prélat,
> Plusieurs chiens mangeaient un potage,
> Mais si pressés autour du plat,
> Qu'il ne se pouvait davantage.
> Un gros mâtin garde-tison,
> Ne cessait pendant ce désordre,
> D'aboyer contre eux et de mordre ;
> Et soulevant les gens de la maison.
> Leur reprochait en son langage,
> Que c'était une trahison,
> D'abandonner le bien de leur maître au pillage.
> Enfin après beaucoup d'éclat,
> Il se rendit maître du plat.
> Mais quand aux étrangers il eût donné la chasse,
> Il se mit bravement à manger à leur place.

MORALITE

> Ainsi dans les guerres civiles,
> Ceux qui des peuples, et des villes,
> Excitent le soulèvement ;
> Quand leurs intrigues leur succèdent,
> Et qu'ils ont le gouvernement,
> Ils font encore pis, que ceux qu'ils dépossèdent.

ANTOINE FURETIÈRE *(1619–1688)*

Many a Hound

In a priest's kitchen, many a hound,
Crowding about a bowl of soup,
Was supping… Pressed so tightly round
Were they, that hardly could the group
Have welcomed one soul more! But lo!
A hearth-guard mastiff tried his best
To wedge his way amongst the rest,
With strident bark and bite… But no!
He could but rouse the household servant-folk,
And, scoffing, in his language, spoke
These words: "How treasonous of you to be
So profligate with Master's property!"
Whereat, after much how-d'ye-do,
He makes the soup his own—and the bowl too!—
Chasing the looters from their feast, a-glut,
And takes their place: no "if", no "and", no "but"!

MORAL

So too, amongst the population,
When civil war divides a nation;
When rebels rise up and defeat
The government that ruled before…
When their intrigues succeed, still more
Unseemly they than those whom they unseat.

JEAN DE LA FONTAINE *(1621–1695)*

Le chien qui lâche sa proie pour l'ombre

Chacun se trompe ici-bas :
On voit courir après l'ombre
Tant de fous, qu'on n'en sait pas
La plupart du temps le nombre.
Au Chien dont parle Esope il faut les renvoyer.
Ce Chien, voyant sa proie en l'eau représentée,
La quitta pour l'image, et pensa se noyer.
La rivière devint tout d'un coup agitée ;
A toute peine il regagna les bords,
Et n'eut ni l'ombre ni le corps.

JEAN DE LA FONTAINE *(1621–1695)*

The Dog Who Drops His Prey for Its Reflection

To err is human. Here below,
Many the folk—or fools—who go
Chasing a shadow; more, indeed,
Than one can count. Best let them read
The tale about a dog that Aesop tells,
Who, by a stream, prey clutched between his teeth,
Eyes its reflection in the waves beneath,
Lunges, falls in. The water swirls and swells.
Near drowned, he struggles back to shore. But oh, the cost:
Shadow and substance both, alas, are lost.

Le chien a qui on a coupé les oreilles

« Qu'ai-je fait, pour me voir ainsi
Mutilé par mon propre maître ?
Le bel état où me voici !
Devant les autres chiens oserai-je paraître ?
Ô rois des animaux, ou plutôt leurs tyrans,
Qui vous ferait choses pareilles ? »
Ainsi criait Mouflar, jeune Dogue ; et les gens,
Peu touchés de ses cris douloureux et perçants,
Venaient de lui couper sans pitié les oreilles.
Mouflar y croyait perdre : il vit avec le temps
Qu'il y gagnait beaucoup ; car étant de nature
A piller ses pareils, mainte mésaventure
L'aurait fait retourner chez lui
Avec cette partie en cent lieux altérée ;
Chien hargneux a toujours l'oreille déchirée.
Le moins qu'on peut laisser de prise aux dents d'autrui
C'est le mieux. Quand on n'a qu'un endroit à défendre,
On le munit, de peur d'esclandre :
Témoin maître Mouflar armé d'un gorgerin,
Du reste ayant d'oreille autant que sur ma main ;
Un Loup n'eût su par où le prendre.

JEAN DE LA FONTAINE *(1621–1695)*

The Dog Who Had His Ears Cut Short

"What have I done to be wronged so,
    And by my master mutilated?
Before my fellow dogs do I dare show
My face, in such a state abbreviated?
Would one do this to you, O Man? You, king
    Of all the beasts? Their king? Nay, nay!
    Rather their tyrant should I say!"
So whined young jowl-hung Hound. Scarce listening,
Those who had clipped his ears paid little mind
To his sharp cries. But, though today he pined
    His loss, in time he was to find
    That he was better thus, so cropped,
    And, on reflection, would have stopped
His sad lament. For he was of a kind
Much given to pillaging his peers, and he
Returned from misadventures frequently
With ears nipped, bitten, rent a hundredfold.
    (For growling dog—so we are told—
Ever sports ragged ear!) Best to expose   *
    The least one can to fearsome foe's
Sharp fangs, lest he a solid tooth-hold take.
    Spike-collared now, young Hound can make
A staunch defense, in one place concentrated.
With no more long ears on his head than I,
    Hound will leave Wolf exasperated:
No longer has he ears to seize him by.

---

*The original cites the proverb *"Chien hargneux a toujours l'oreille déchirée"* (A growling dog always has a ragged ear).

29

CHARLES PERRAULT *(1628–1703)*

Le chien, le coq et le renard

Le chien, avec un coq, entreprit un voyage ;
D'abord dans un même arbre ils passèrent la nuit.
  Le coq monta sur les plus hauts branchages ;
Le chien dans le trou creux établit son réduit.
  Dès le matin le coq fit son ramage ;
Aussitôt un renard, de bonne heure éveillé,
Vint à lui, le pria de vouloir bien descendre,
Disant que de son chant surpris, émerveillé,
  Plus longuement il ne pouvait attendre,
Qu'il voulait embrasser l'aimable musicien
Qui venait de chanter et de chanter si bien.
Le coq, qui reconnut sa louange traitresse,
    Lui dit avec la même adresse :
    « Je n'ai pas de plus grand désir
    Que de vous donner du plaisir ;
    Mais, si vous voulez que je sorte,
    Il faut éveiller le portier,
    Afin qu'il nous ouvre la porte ;
    Oserai-je vous en prier ? »
Le chien au premier coup sortit de sa demeure ;
Le malheureux renard pensa mourir de peur ;
Il fuit, le chien le prit et l'étrangla sur l'heure.

C'est le vrai droit du jeu de tromper le trompeur.

CHARLES PERRAULT *(1628–1703)*

The Dog, the Cock, and the Fox

A dog and cock, deciding they will go
Traveling a bit, together, find a tree,
Settle in for the night, comfortably,
Cock in the topmost branches, dog below,
Nether-lodged in a hole… At dawn's first light,
    Cock doodles his *cocorico,*   *
    Waking a wily fox, who—oh,
So covetous of cock—a-trot, slinks right
    Up to their tree… "Ah, would I might,
Here, on the spot, embrace you, songster rare!"
    He begs cock to come down from where
He perches. "Gladly," his reply. But cock's
Wiles are no less than fox's. "Dear friend fox,
Surely will I come down and pleasure you.
First, though, you must wake our concierge." "Your who?"
"The doorman…" "Oh…" Two knocks and, from his lair,
    Dog leaps, claws fox, near dead from fear,
Strangling him in his clutches, ear to ear.

To cheat the cheat: what fairer rule is there!

---

* *"Cocorico"* is the traditional French approximation of the cock's crow, equivalent of the English "cock-a-doodle-doo".

Le chien Gascon

Je suis de la fidélité,
Disait un chien, le vrai symbole.
Combien de trésors ont été
Sous ma tutelle en sûreté,
Sans que j'en ôtasse une obole !
Est-il d'animal comme moi,
En souplesse qui me surpasse,
Lorsque, devant le jeune roi,
Je fais des tours de passe-passe ?
Je vous détaillerais mon art
Et pour la chasse et pour la pêche
Où je nage comme un canard ;
Mais ma modestie en empêche.
Savez-vous ce que répondit
Une jeune éperlan femelle :
Que n'ai-je au moins une parcelle
De tous les talents qu'il décrit !
Voici ma vie ; écoutez, belle :
On m'enfile, et puis on me frit.

JEAN-BAPTISTE-JOSEPH WILLART DE GRÉCOURT
(1684–1743)

The Gascon Dog   *

Boastful, a dog proclaimed: "I am
Loyalty's symbol. Aye, the very
Picture of honesty, madame…   **
How many a treasure legendary
Lay in my care, without one gram
Tempting me to make free with it!
Is there an animal like me,
Supple of form, more lithe and fit,
When, for the young king, cleverly,
I do my tricks? How exquisite,
My dextrous prestidigitation!
If modesty allowed, I would,
Without the least exaggeration,
Describe my talents, tell how good
I am at hunting, fishing, swimming—
Duck-like!—with arts aquatic brimming!…"
At that, a female smelt pipes up:
"Pray give ear to that braggart pup!
Why have I not one whit, my dear,
Of his skills? Why must they deny me!
As for me, life is dull, I fear:
They hook me, pull me in… and fry me!"

---

* Inhabitants of Gascony are considered by the French to be inveterate braggarts.

** My "madame", not in the original, gives a glimpse of the dog's smelt-interlocutor—
the *"jeune éperlan femelle"*—introduced at the end of the poem.

JEAN-BAPTISTE-JOSEPH WILLART DE GRÉCOURT
(1684–1743)

Le petit chien

Un petit chien se montrait à la foire,
Et par l'esprit, l'adresse et la mémoire
De certains tours, s'y faisait admirer,
Grande fortune il aurait pu tirer
De ses talents ; mais dissipé, volage,
Toujours était ailleurs qu'à son ouvrage.
Allons tout droit, et sautez pour le roi,
Lui disait-on. Le drôle restait coi,
Point ne sautait. Sautez donc pour la reine
L'ordre donné, la menace était vaine.
Venez à moi. Zeste, bien loin de là
Il s'enfuyait. Je sais d'où vient cela.
        Dites-lui ; sautez pour follette ;
        Et vous verrez un joli saut.
        L'esprit est souvent en défaut,
        Nature n'est jamais distraite.

JEAN-BAPTISTE-JOSEPH WILLART DE GRÉCOURT
  (1684–1743)

The Little Pup

A little pup there was, who, at the fair—
Possessed of wit and skill *extraordinaire*—
Served up amazing feats, many of which
Might well have earned for him a fortune rich
Beyond compare. But lax and unconcerned,
    At length, he turned his head and spurned
Commands. As when they said: "Jump for the king!"
    Whereat the curious little thing
Stood pat… "Well then, jump for the queen!" they said…
Again, "No!" growled the lazy quadruped…
At last, "Come here, pet!…" Humbug! He would fly,
Fleeing afar!… And, should you wonder why,
Tell him: "Jump for the spicy little bitch!"
And you will see him leap! High… High… For, though
    Wit can spell Man a headstrong "No!"
    Always must Nature scratch her itch!

NICOLAS GROZELIER *(1692–1778)*

Le chien qui aboie à la lune   *

      Dans la nuit, un chien aboyait
    Contre la lune, et lui chantait injure,
    Et cependant elle continuait
       A répandre sa clarté pure ;
    Lorsqu'un cheval, que le mâtin gardait ;
       S'ennuyant du bruit qu'il faisait,
Lui dit : crois-tu pouvoir obscurcir la lumière
       Du bel astre qui nous éclaire.
Pauvre animal, tes cris sont impuissants,
Tais-toi, tu perds et ta peine et ton temps.

      Contre l'honneur du vrai mérite,
      La jalousie en vain s'irrite ;
Et pour la diffamer, forme maint attentat :
Le mérite attaqué brille avec plus d'éclat.

---

* Every translator, especially of poetry, realizes that translation is the art and craft of choice. Choice of a word, a phrase, a rhyme, a metric figure… And even of an entire version. Occasionally I decide to do more than one version of the same original. As with the present trifle. And, rather than choose one over the other, I take the liberty of offering both to the reader.

   One night, a dog would bark against
The moon, with insults hurled hard as he might.
    Stubborn, the orb, uninfluenced,
Stood firm, dispensed no less her clear, pure light.

NICOLAS GROZELIER *(1692–1778)*

The Hound Who Bays at the Moon

A hound bays at the moon one night. His tune?
A whining howl, a growled cacophony,
    Hoping, thereby, he might impugn
Her shining rays. But, unaffected, she
Sheds the same light in utter purity,
    And spreads it round no less… Now, soon,
A horse, entrusted to the mastiff's care,
Irked by the noise, neighs: "Why must you sit there,
Barking against the star that shines on us?
    Be still! The more you fume and fuss,
The more you waste your breath! Beast, best beware!"

True merit all too often is attacked
    By envy. But in vain… In fact,
Do what one will to quell its quality,
Talent, attacked, shines the more brilliantly.

    A horse—far more experienced
    Than his hound-guard—unnerved, incensed
At all his noise, asked: "Do you think that, thus,
You can dull that chaſte ſtar that shines on us?
Poor beaſt! Your cries are vain! No good they do!
Be ſtill! You waſte your time, and trouble too!"

It makes no sense when jealousy speaks ill,
    Wreaks its wrath on true merit. For,
    Merit, attacked, will all the more
Stand faſt, and caſt its brilliance, brighter ſtill.

NICOLAS GROZELIER *(1692–1778)*

Le fermier et ses quatre chiens

Vive les conseils des vieillards :
Il n'est rien tel à tous égards,
Surtout en fait d'économie,
Et s'il s'agit de conserver sa vie.

Un gros fermier avait quatre chiens vigoureux
Pour défendre la bergerie,
Et pour garder sa métairie.
Chaque jour les plus forts d'entr'eux
Faisaient aux loups si bonne guerre,
Qu'il n'en paraissait presque plus.
Un soir qu'ils étaient revenus
Tout triomphants de leur chasse ordinaire,
Les deux chiens plus âgés leur dirent en colère :
En détruisant ainsi les loups,
Têtes folles, qu'allez-vous faire ?
Vous nous portez les derniers coups.
Quand le fermier n'aura plus rien à craindre
Pour ses moutons, il nous chassera tous.
Modérez votre ardeur, et sachez vous contraindre.

NICOLAS GROZELIER *(1692–1778)*

The Farmer and His Four Dogs

Hurrah for elders' wise advice!
We cannot place a worldly price
Upon its worth, especially
If we would live life, long, disaster-free.

A wealthy farmer kept four guard-dogs, whose
Task it was to protect his crops, his sheep,
From the marauding felons' stealth and ruse,
The wolves', that is! Two earned so well their keep—
The youngest, most robust—and waged such war
    Against the wolfly predator,
That there remained only a paltry few…
One night, returning from a raid, our pair,
Having once more laid low the enemy lair,
    Was challenged by the elder two:
"*Chers frères!* Poor fools, you know not what you do!
When safe his sheep, with no more wolves to fear,
    When their last remnants disappear,
What will the master have to do with you?
Nothing! Our fate is in your claws. And thus,

Moins n'en disait un de nos vieux guerriers
A son fils, jeune encor, trop friand de lauriers :
A quoi te servira de prendre tant de villes ?
C'est vouloir travailler à nous rendre inutiles :
Si tu vas de ce train, on pourra bien chez nous
        Nous renvoyer planter des choux.

Best you hear what an ancient conqueror
Once told his warrior son, who hungered for
The hero's life, ever victorious:
'Your exploits render us superfluous!
Useless are we! And, as the proverb says:
We might as well go plant our cabbages!'"   *

---

* Montaigne's allusion to the nobility of "planting one's cabbages" in the face of death (*Les Essais,* 1595, I, 20), while not a proverb, has achieved a kind of proverbial status thanks to its frequently quoted echo in the celebrated last words of Voltaire's *Candide* (1759): "… but let us cultivate our garden."

CHRISTIAN GELLERT *(1715–1769)*

Le chien fidèle

Certain larron connu par maints bons tours
Et surnommé Docteur parmi ses camarades
Sur les biens d'un chanoine avait jeté ses grades,
La nuit précipitait son cours ;
Gros Jean le sommelier, Margot la chambrière,
Tout avait fermé la paupière,
Le maître du logis ronflait profondément
Et semblait au voleur indiquer le moment.
Un dogue seul veillait, gardien trop fidèle,
Le larron lui jeta du pain ;
Tu t'abuses beaucoup, lui dit la sentinelle,
Si tu crois m'engager à servir ton dessein ;
Ta libéralité m'avertit au contraire
D'éveiller le maître et ses gens,
Ce pain-là sent la harde et n'est pas mon affaire.

Laocoon disait à peu près en ce sens,
Je crains les Grecs et leurs présents.

CHRISTIAN GELLERT *(1715–1769)*

The Faithful Hound

A certain thief there was, renowned as one
Most versed in arts of thievery—the very
Chief of all thiefdom's minions exemplary!—
Who coveted a churchman's wealth. The sun,
One night, had run its course as, dark and deep,
 Behind the heavy lids of sleep,
The household—everyone and everything—
Lay still: Gros Jean the steward, Dame Margot.
The lot!… The master too lay bellowing
 Slumber's snored sounds profound. And so
Thief thought it was his time to strike. All round,
No wakeful eyes… Save, that is, for a hound
 On faithful watch… Just then, although
Thief flings a chunk of bread his way, "You err,"
Dog barks. "Naught will I do, you scurvy cur,
But wake Monsieur and all his retinue,
To come and lay you low without ado!
Fie on your trick! A fig for your fine wit!
Your bread reeks of the leash. I'll none of it!"

I fear Greeks bearing gifts. Laocoön
It was who so opined, oft and anon. *

---

* In the *Aeneid* (II, 49) Virgil gives the priest Laocoön the line *"Timeo Danaos et dona ferentes"* ("I fear the Greeks, even bearing gifts"), as he tries, unsuccessfully, to persuade the Trojans to reject the gift of the celebrated wooden horse that would prove their undoing.

PRINCE IGNACY KRASICKI *(1735–1801)*

Les deux chiens

« Quoi ! Je gèle au grand air, et tu dors au salon ? »
Disait le chien de cour au Mopse du bon ton.
« La raison, dit le Mopse, est simple, ou je m'abuse ;
En deux mots la voici : tu sers, et moi j'amuse. »

PRINCE IGNACY KRASICKI *(1735–1801)*

The Two Dogs

Farm dog asks lapdog pug in tête-à-tête,   *
"Why do I freeze, while you, rich, pampered pet,
In salon comfort sleep!" "Let me explain.
You serve the master. Me? I entertain."

* The poet contrasts the outdoor *chien de cour*, equivalent of the Italian *cane corso*, with the lapdog *carlin—Möpse* in German—favorite of elegant 19th-century society ladies.

PRINCE IGNACY KRASICKI *(1735–1801)*

Le chien et le chasseur

Un chien quitta son maître. Ayant erré deux jours,
Il trouva sire loup, implora son secours,
      Et fut admis à son service.
Il prit lièvres, chevreuils ; la chasse était propice.
Toujours nouveau butin, dévoré par le loup ;
« Oh ! dit le chien, ceci ne me plaît pas beaucoup :
Rien chez vous, Monseigneur, à profit ne me tourne ;
      Mon ancien maître me rossait,
      Mais au moins il me nourrissait :
Adieu donc ; sans tarder à l'homme je retourne ! »

PRINCE IGNACY KRASICKI *(1735–1801)*

The Hound and the Hunter   *

A hound, quitting his master, wandered round,
Two days on end, until Sir Wolf he found,
    Begged that, to serve the latter's need,
    He take him in. The wolf agreed…
The hunt was good: hound took his share of hind,
    Of hare—fresh game of every kind,
No sooner captured than by wolf devoured.
"Zounds!" complains hound. "I fear my zeal has soured.
Never a meal? I labor fruitlessly!
    My master pummeled me, 'tis true,
    But still, at least he fed me too!
Adieu, dear beast. It's back to Man with me!"

---

* Although "The Hound and the Wolf" would be a better choice of title, since no hunter appears in the original, I translate the title as given in my source, but I cannot vouch for its accuracy.

JEAN-JACQUES-FRANÇOIS-MARIN BOISARD
(1744–1813)

Le bonze et le chien

       Un Bonze fut mordu d'un Chien.
Il pouvoit riposter par un coup de massue ;
     Il se vengea par un autre moyen:
« Ma loi ne permet pas, » dit-il, « que je te tue ;
Je ne te tuerai pas, mais tu n'y perdras rien ;
Et je vais te donner mauvaise renommée. »
       Il tient parole, & dans l'instant
Crie: « au Chien enragé » ; le peuple en fait autant ;
Estafiers d'accourir, la bête est assommée.

JEAN-JACQUES-FRANÇOIS-MARIN BOISARD
(1744–1813)

The Buddhist Monk and the Hound

A hound, they tell us, bit a priest
(A Buddhist monk, that is, come from the East),
Who would have countered with a cudgel-blow.
But no. "My law lets me not kill," he said.
"I'll take revenge by speaking ill instead."
And so he cries: "Mad dog! Mad dog!" "Oh, oh!"
Echo the folk, in fear and dread,
Beating to death our quadruped, who, lo!
Lies no less cudgeled now… And no less dead.   *

---

* Boisard's monk is merely heeding the advice of an old French proverb: *Qui veut noyer son chien l'accuse de la rage.* Its medieval equivalent is traceable at least as far back as the thirteenth century: *"Qui bon chien veut tuer, la raige li met seur"*—that is, if you want an excuse to kill your dog, just say that he is rabid. See Antoine-Jean-Victor Le Roux de Lincy, *Le Livre des proverbes français,* I:109. The proverb also provides the moral for one of the Aesopic fables in the medieval collection *Isopet I de Paris.* See "The Wolf and the Lamb," in my *Fables from Old French: Aesop's Beasts and Bumpkins,* p. 55.

ANTOINE VITALLIS *(1749–1830)*

Le petit chien

L'enfant le plus choyé, toujours est le plus sot.

Un petit chien, empâté de biscuit,
  De fin bonbon et de gimblettes,
Étouffait d'embonpoint. Partout il n'était bruit
  Que de sa graisse et de ce qui s'ensuit :
Car des talents ! Aucun. Or, sur ces entrefaites,
  Sa vieille maîtresse mourut ;
  Et dans les parts qui furent faites
  De ses écus, de ses cornettes,
Et du singe, et du chat, et de toutes ses bêtes,
  Favori, par hasard, échut
  A la plus vilaine qui fut,
  Des trois nièces de la défunte.
  Plus de biscuits, encor moins de bonbon ;
  Du pain tout sec ; si faut-il qu'on l'emprunte,
Bien dur, à la voisine, alors qu'à la maison
  Il est trop frais, partant trop bon.
  Favori se fit avec peine
  A cet ordinaire frugal,
   Et grâce à la vilaine
  Qui le traitait si mal,
Sa graisse disparut en moins d'une semaine ;
  Mais il y gagna la santé,
   L'agilité,

ANTOINE VITALLIS *(1749–1830)*

The Little Dog

Pamper a child and hamper his good sense.

Little dog Favori, biscuit-stuffed pup,
 Relished the many tasty treats
His mistress fed him, fattening him up
 On savory scones and fine sweetmeats,
Till, when one spoke of him, "How fat!" was all
One said! "Alas! He cannot last, withal!"
His talents? Not a one!… Now then, one day,
 His agèd mistress passed away,
And when came time to dole her legacy
 To her close kin, her nieces three
 Gave ear to hear the lucky legatee.   *
Who gets her wealth, her headdresses? Who gets
Her cat, her monkey, all her household pets?
And Favori the Fat?… This last bequest
 Went, by chance, to the stingiest
Of the three. Never, now, a scone, a sweet,
Nothing but hard, stale bread no one would eat,
 And that the neighbor lady gave her…
Favori? He consumed the frugal fare,
 Became, in fact, slender and spare,
   Gaining in favor,
   Losing in fat,

---

*   I follow the original's somewhat unorthodox use of a single rhyme over three successive lines.

Et surtout l'amabilité
　　Tout fut donc pour le mieux.
　　Ce chien me représente
Un enfant qu'on a dorloté,
Et qui doit plus en vérité,
Au dur pédant qui le régente,
Qu'aux sots parents qui l'ont gâté.

More agile too… And that was that.
Everything for the best, or so they say.   **
I see this dog the symbol of
The child pampered by parents' love
And who—harsh pedant's *protégé*—
Owes more to switch that rapped and roiled him
Than to the parent-fools who spoiled him.

** This line appears without a rhyme in the original. I can't resist the temptation of providing one in my translation.

JEAN-PIERRE CLARIS DE FLORIAN *(1755–1794)*

Le chien coupable

> Mon frère, sais-tu la nouvelle ?
Mouflar, le bon Mouflar, de nos chiens, le modèle,
Si redouté des loups, si soumis au berger,
> Mouflar vient, dit-on, de manger
Le petit agneau noir, puis la brebis sa mère,
Et puis sur le berger s'est jeté furieux.
> —Serait-il vrai ? —Très vrai, mon frère.
> —A qui donc se fier, grands dieux ! »

C'est ainsi que parlaient deux moutons dans la plaine.
> Et la nouvelle était certaine.
> Mouflar, sur le fait même, pris,
> N'attendait plus que le supplice ;
Et le fermier voulait qu'une prompte justice
> Effrayât les chiens du pays.

> La procédure en un jour est finie.
Mille témoins pour un, déposent l'attentat.
Récolés, confrontés, aucun d'eux ne varie :
Mouflar est convaincu du triple assassinat.

Mouflar recevra donc deux balles dans la tête
> Sur le lieu même du délit.
> À son supplice qui s'apprête,
> Toute la ferme se rendit.

JEAN-PIERRE CLARIS DE FLORIAN *(1755–1794)*

The Guilty Hound

"Brother mine, have you heard the news?
Gentle Mouflar, our guardian-hound… He whose
 Glory surpasses all the rest…
 Mouflar, our shepherd's truest, best,
Most fearsome foe of wolves…" "Indeed…" "He who
Panics them…" "So?" "The story goes that he
Devoured the black sheep, then its mother ewe…
Even struck dead the shepherd!…" "Can it be?"
 "Quite so!" "Good gods above! I vow!
 Who knows who's to be trusted now!"

So spoke two sheep grazing the meadow grass.
 And the event? Too true, alas!
Mouflar, caught in the act, now prisoner pent—
Disgraced, before the flock-tribunal lying,
Picture of farmer's justice terrifying—
Waited to bear his swift, sure punishment.

The trial lasts but a day. The witnesses—
Some thousand—hold to their corroboration.
 "Guilty, no question!" each one says.
"Guilty of the threefold assassination!"

The sentence? There, even upon the dread
 Site of his crime, the hound will be
 Dispatched: two bullets to the head!
 From round the farm, all came to see.

Les agneaux de Mouflar demandèrent la grâce.
Elle fut refusée. On leur fit prendre place.
       Les chiens se rangèrent près d'eux,
Tristes, humiliés, mornes, l'oreille basse,
Plaignant, sans l'excuser, leur frère malheureux.

Tout le monde attendait dans un profond silence.
Mouflar paraît bientôt, conduit par deux pasteurs :
Il arrive ; et, levant au ciel ses yeux en pleurs,
       Il harangue ainsi l'assistance :

« Ô vous, qu'en ce moment je n'ose et je ne puis
Nommer comme autrefois, mes frères, mes amis,
       Témoins de mon heure dernière,
Voyez où peut conduire un coupable désir !
De la vertu, quinze ans j'ai suivi la carrière.
       Un faux pas m'en a fait sortir.

« Apprenez mes forfaits. Au lever de l'aurore,
Seul, auprès du grand bois, je gardais le troupeau.
       Un loup vient, emporte un agneau,
       Et tout en fuyant le dévore.
Je cours, j'atteins le loup, qui, laissant son festin,
       Vient m'attaquer : je le terrasse,
       Et je l'étrangle sur la place.

« C'était bien jusque là : mais, pressé par la faim,
De l'agneau dévoré, je regarde le reste,
J'hésite, je balance… À la fin, cependant,
       J'y porte une coupable dent :
Voilà de mes malheurs l'origine funeste.

His lambs rose, pled for mercy. "Nay," replied
The court, bleating them down. And, by their side,
The other dogs, humiliated, lay,
Ears a-droop, glum, pitying him, though they
Could not excuse his heinous homicide.

Everyone waits… Silence profound…
Mouflar, led by two shepherds, bound, appears,
Eyes heavenward and bathed in tears.
At length, thus rants our captive hound:

"O you, whom I may now no longer name
My friends and brothers, who witness my shame
Sharing my final hour this day…
See where one foul desire can lead us to.
For fifteen years I trod the virtuous way,
Now one false step has turned my life askew.

"Pray hear my sins… One daybreak, there I am,
Alone, by woodland's edge, guarding *ad hoc*
My sheep… A wolf appears, ogles the flock…
Suddenly seizes one young lamb,
Makes off, devouring it… I leap, give chase,
Catch him… He drops his prey… The vile scapegrace
Attacks me… I fight back, lay the beast low…
Strangle him where he lies, just so.

"So far, so good. But, famished, I see—spread
Temptingly—the poor lamb's remains… Alas!
To eat or not to eat?… Yes? No?… No? Yes?…
Why not? What difference? Dead is dead!

« La brebis vient dans cet instant,
Elle jette des cris de mère…
La tête m'a tourné, j'ai craint que la brebis
Ne m'accusât d'avoir assassiné son fils.
Et, pour la forcer à se taire,
Je l'égorge dans ma colère.

« Le berger accourait armé de son bâton.
N'espérant plus aucun pardon,
Je me jette sur lui : mais bientôt on m'enchaîne,
Et me voici prêt à subir
De mes crimes, la juste peine.

« Apprenez tous du moins, en me voyant mourir,
Que la plus légère injustice,
Aux forfaits les plus grands peut conduire d'abord ;
Et que, dans le chemin du vice,
On est au fond du précipice,
Dès qu'on met un pied sur le bord. »

And, in the end, if you would know the truth,
I sink into its flesh a guilty tooth.

     "Just then, the ewe approaches. She
     Weeps, wails a mother's piteous cries…
I lose my head… I fear lest she blame me
For murdering her son before her eyes,
And, to assure her silence, I cannot
But choose to slay her, throat slit on the spot.

"Next moment, comes the shepherd, running, stick
In hand… Fled now all hope of pardon! Quick,
     Undone, I leap, lunge, do him in!…
Soon, bound and chained, a prisoner here I lie,
Waiting to suffer for my triple sin.

     "Seeing me thus about to die,
Learn, at least, that along the road of vice,
'Once', in an instant, may well lead to 'thrice'!
Put one foot on the rim of the abyss!
Soon must you plunge over the precipice!"

JEAN-PIERRE CLARIS DE FLORIAN *(1755–1794)*

La brebis et le chien

La brebis et le chien, de tous les temps amis,
Se racontaient un jour leur vie infortunée.
—Ah ! disait la brebis, je pleure et je frémis
Quand je songe aux malheurs de notre destinée.

Toi, l'esclave de l'homme, adorant des ingrats,
          Toujours soumis, tendre et fidèle,
          Tu reçois, pour prix de ton zèle,
          Des coups et souvent le trépas.

          Moi, qui tous les ans les habille,
Qui leur donne du lait, et qui fume leurs champs,
Je vois chaque matin quelqu'un de ma famille
          Assassiné par ces méchants.

Leurs confrères, les loups, dévorent ce qu'il reste.
          Victimes de ces inhumains,
Travailler pour eux seuls, et mourir par leurs mains,
          Voilà notre destin funeste !

—Il est vrai, dit le chien, mais crois-tu plus heureux
          Les auteurs de notre misère ?
          Va, ma sœur, il vaut encore mieux
          Souffrir le mal que de le faire.

JEAN-PIERRE CLARIS DE FLORIAN *(1755–1794)*

The Ewe and the Dog

Good friends for many a year, a dog and sheep—
A ewe—one day were chatting aimlessly.
The latter moaned: "I shudder and I weep
When I muse on our lives' cruel destiny.

"You, mankind's selfless slave, who, with each breath,
    Worship your thankless masters, who
      Repay your loyal love, askew,
      With kick and blow… and, often, death.

    "Me, who—though I provide them with
Their clothes, their milk, spread dung to fertilize
Their fields—must see one of my kin and kith,
    Each day, done in before my eyes!

"Their wolf *confrères* glut on what's left of us,
    Undone by their inhuman band.
We slave for man yet perish by his hand:
    Such, our fate ignominious!"

"True," says dog. "But, best we not misconstrue it.
    Are evildoers happy? When
      Evil is done, with dogs like men:
    Better to suffer it than do it."

ADELINE JOLIVEAU DE SEGRAIS *(1756–1830)*

L'éducation tardive

Je te ferai mourir sous le bâton,
Dit un maître au pauvre Fidèle ;
Ne pourras-tu jamais, comme un chien du bon ton,
Faire la révérence, et me prouvant ton zèle,
Gambader pour Monsieur, pour Madame sauter,
Puis élégamment rapporter ?
Tu ne seras jamais qu'une faible cervelle.
—Hélas ! Mon maître, j'en conviens ;
Je ne suis pas le plus adroit des chiens ;
Cependant, si dès ma jeunesse,
(Ne vous offensez pas de cette liberté) ;
Vous m'eussiez mieux instruit dans la maturité,
Je pourrais montrer plus d'adresse,
Plaire par quelque gentillesse ;
Mais déjà manquant de souplesse,
Mes membres se sont endurcis.

De notre chien la raison était bonne :
Dès le printemps, cultivez donc vos fruits,
Si vous voulez en jouir dans l'automne.

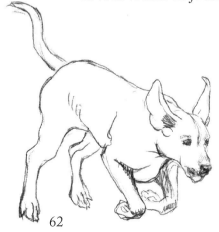

ADELINE JOLIVEAU DE SEGRAIS *(1756–1830)*

A Lesson Too Late

"I should beat you to death, faithless Fidele!   *
     Why must you disobey, ignore me?
     Why, stubborn dog, must you rebel"
     Will you not bow your head before me,
     Like other dogs of breeding fine;
     Go fetch, like proper-bred canine;
     Jump for Monsieur, frisk for Madame?
     You are, mean wretch, a mindless cur,
     And evermore shall be!" "Good sir,
     I fear I must confess I am
     Quite what you say. But try, I pray,
     To understand the reason why.
     Grown old, no longer lithe and spry
Am I! When I was young, dear master—may
     I be so bold to offer my
Opinion!—such, the time you might have taught
     The skills an elder canine ought
Display! But now, I am much too grown up
     To learn, alas! And, even if
You sought to teach, my limbs are cold and stiff…"

Fidele spoke true: sage, now, the erstwhile pup!
If you would savor autumn's harvesting,
Best sow your favor's seedlings in the spring!

---

* I can't resist the irony—not expressed in the original—of having the ill-tempered master in my version pair "Fidele" with its opposite, "faithless", an example of the sort of defensible liberty a translator—this one, at least—finds himself taking.

Le mauvais chien

Un maître suspendit un jour, une clochette,
Sous le cou de son chien qui mordait les passants,
    Pour avertir qu'on fît prompte retraite.
Lui, de se rengorger, de se battre les flancs :
—De ma vertu, dit-il, voici la récompense ;
Et quelqu'un indigné : —Tu te trompes, cruel ;
Ce signe, de ton maître est un trait de prudence ;
Il annonce à chacun ton mauvais naturel.

La clochette irait bien, je pense, à tel et tel.

ADELINE JOLIVEAU DE SEGRAIS *(1756–1830)*

The Cruel Hound

A master hangs a tinkling bell, one day,
From his hound's neck, because—fierce biter, he!—
Best all be warned lest they might pass his way.
The beast, a-strut, delights arrogantly:
"See how they prize my worth!" "Preposterous!"
Another cries: "You err, you stupid cur, you!
Your master, wise, merely tries to deter you
From your cruel nature ignominious!"

That tinkling bell could well serve most of us.

ANTOINE-VINCENT ARNAULT *(1766–1834)*

Le chien et les puces

A-t-on des puces, mes amis,
Il faut songer à s'en défaire.
Mais loin qu'il fût de cet avis,
Certain barbet jadis faisait tout le contraire,
Et du ton d'un riche, ou d'un grand
Qui s'enorgueillirait des amis de tout rang,
Dont toute bonne table en tout pays foisonne,
Disait, au lieu de se gratter :
« Que de gens je puis me flatter
D'avoir autour de ma personne !
Un peuple tout entier accompagne mes pas. »
« Rien de plus vrai, » dit une puce ;
« Mais, crois-moi, ne t'en prévaux pas :
S'il tient à toi, c'est qu'il te suce. »

ANTOINE-VINCENT ARNAULT *(1766–1834)*

The Dog and the Fleas

Do you have fleas? Find a good stratagem,
    My friend—if you want my advice—
    Please, to be promptly rid of them,
    Like any other loathsome lice!
A spaniel cur fancied the opposite,
Thinking himself a *grand seigneur,* to be
Surrounded by a fawning company
Whom he oft wined-and-dined as might befit
His station… Thus instead of scratching, he
Opined: "You must admit, O lucky me!…"
"Exaggeration!" says a flea. "No doubt, you
    Have little cause to thank your luck!
Your wealth is not what draws us all about you:
Your blood alone is what we seek to suck!"

MARC-LOUIS DE TARDY *(1769–1857)*

Le chien et le chat

Castor, jeune épagneul rempli de gentillesse,
  Etait nourri dans la même maison
Avec un certain chat qu'on appelait Minon.
Minon, sous des dehors tout pleins de politesse,
  Savait cacher l'humeur de son espèce ;
  Avec le chien il prenait son ébat ;
  Même coussin leur servait de couchette,
  Et tous les deux mangeaient au même plat.
Un jour il arriva, quand la soupe fut prête,
   Que l'épagneul en goguette
  S'avisa de crier : « Au rat! »
Et Minon de courir pendant que son confrère,
  Plus affamé qu'à l'ordinaire,
  A lui tout seul avalait le dîner.
Bien plus, lorsque Minon arriva de sa quête,
D'un grand éclat de rire il lui partit au nez.
L'animal cauteleux prit mal ce badinage,
Et, se voyant privé de rat et de potage,
D'un coup de griffe à l'œil il marqua bel et bien
   Le pauvre chien.
Castor, tout parafé, se désespère; il crie.
Lors, pour le consoler, la servante qui rit :
  « Monsieur Castor, on vous l'avait bien dit :
Avec mauvaises gens point de plaisanterie. »

MARC-LOUIS DE TARDY *(1769 –1857)*

The Dog and the Cat

Castor, young spaniel, pleasant as you please,
Lived in a home that housed as well a cat—
Minon by name—whose outward qualities
Bespoke tame tenderness… But, for all that,
 There dwelt within his feline skin
The same beast common to his cat-folk kin!
 The two disported, slept, and ate,
Each in the other's company: one plate,
One pillow served them both… Now then, one day,
 Just as their soup was set before
 The pair, devil-may-care Castor
 Takes it into his head to say:
"Look!… See?… A rat!…" Whereat his fleet confrere
Goes dashing off to snatch the would-be snare,
 Leaving our hungry pup to sup
The soup, and, all alone, lap it all up!
Back snarls Minon, much abashed from his quest—
Rat-less, of course! Castor, proud of his jest,
Snickers a sneer. Thereat, our cunning cat—
 Having now neither soup nor rat!—
Lashes out at our dog with swoop and swipe.
Castor, snout raw, claw-striped, shrieks his dismay.
At which, the serving-wench, to calm, console him,
Warns with a laugh (more fit to chaff, cajole him!):
  "You feckless popinjay!
You should have learned, poor dog, best not to joke
So recklessly with such ill-tempered folk!"

Le chien, le lapin et le chasseur

César, chien d'arrêt renommé,
Mais trop enflé de son mérite,
Tenait arrêté dans son gîte
Un malheureux lapin de peur inanimé.
Rends-toi, lui cria-t-il d'une voix de tonnerre,
Qui fit au loin trembler les peuplades des bois.
Je suis César, connu par ses exploits,
Et dont le nom remplit toute la terre.
A ce grand nom, Jeannot lapin
Recommandant à Dieu son âme pénitente
Demande d'une voix tremblante :
Très sérénissime mâtin,
Si je me rends, quel sera mon destin ?
—Tu mourras. —Je mourrai ! dit la bête innocente,
Et si je fuis ? —Ton trépas est certain.
—Quoi ! reprit l'animal qui se nourrit de thym,
Des deux côtés je dois perdre la vie ?
Que votre illustre seigneurie
Veuille me pardonner, puisqu'il me faut mourir,

NAPOLÉON BONAPARTE *(1769–1821)*

The Hound, the Rabbit, and the Hunter *

César, a bold retriever of renown,
Full of himself and of his hunting skill—
    Stock-still, had cornered and pinned down
A rabbit in his hole. Tasting the kill,
The hound stood fast before his hapless victim.
"Give yourself up!" he growled with thunderous cry,
    Filled with the haughty pride that pricked him,
Setting the forest folk a-shudder. "I...
I am César! Known round the land for my
Valorous exploits!" At his name, Jeannot,   **
Commending unto God his sinful soul,
Penitent, sighs, a-tremble in his hole:
    "Brave mastiff *serenissimo,*   ***
If I give up, what shall become of me?"
"You die!" "And if I flee?" "Flee? Flee?... Ho ho!
    Surely no less dead shall you be!"
The rabbit, nibbling on a sprig of thyme,

---

* The young Napoléon's authorship of this fable is well established. See *The Literary Gazette: A Weekly Journal of Literature, Science, and the Fine Arts,* August 1, 1857, p. 732, as well as the reference to Joseph-Marie Quérard's assertion in his *Les Bonaparte et leurs œuvres littéraires* (Paris, F. Daguin, 1845) in http://www.Shanaweb.net, le Chien, le Lapin, et le Chasseur.

** "Jeannot" has long been a traditional French name for the rabbit.
*** I suspect that the rabbit is not enough of a Latinist to be offended that I do not have him use the vocative, *serenissime,* in addressing the hound.

Si j'ose tenter de m'enfuir.
—Il dit et fuit, en héros de garenne.
Caton l'aurait blâmé : je dis qu'il n'eut pas tort,
Car le chasseur le voit a peine
Qu'il l'ajuste, le tire… Et le chien tombe mort !
Que dirait de ceci notre bon La Fontaine ?
Aide-toi, le ciel t'aidera.
J'approuve fort cette morale-là.

Exclaims: "Pardon me, sire, I see no rhyme
    Or reason… Since I die… Or die!…
Excuse my quibbling if, at least, I try."
    (Cato, illustrious *philosophe,*
Might blame him. I would not!) And off
He scampers through the wood. The hunter, then—
Dim-eyed—aims, fires, and, missing, hits the hound,
    Who dies before he hits the ground!
    What would say our good La Fontaine?
    "Heaven will help you. But first you
Must help yourself!" I like that moral too.   ****

****La Fontaine's version of this proverbial moral is from his fable "Le Chartier embourbé" (VI, 18). For a translation, see "The Wagoner Caught in the Mud," in my collection *The Complete Fables of Jean de La Fontaine,* Urbana, University of Illinois Press, 2007, pp. 146–47. Incidentally, the Emperor did not have unrestrained admiration for La Fontaine, especially as a children's poet. See the passage from teen-age "Betsy" (Lucie Elizabeth) Balcombe's memoirs of her curious friendship with him during his exile on St-Helena, quoted in http://www. Shanaweb.net (see note above).

JEAN-JOSEPH-MARIUS DIOULOUFET *(1771–1840)*

Lou tigre et lou chin

Un Tigre mangeo un cerf, piey accuso lou Chin ;
Aquo dins la forest faguet bruech et grand trin ;
Qui va cres, va cres pas, et la cavo es pourtado
       Davant leis assisos dou lien,
       Et l'y fouguet que trop prouvado
Que lou Tigre a coumes esto marrido actien.
    De groupatas qu'avien vis lou carnagi
Fougueroun leis temoins que leis cerfs prouduisien ;
Mais lou Tigre a d'amis et quauque parentagi ;
       Entre leis jugis fan partit,
    Voueloun sauvar aquestou persounnagi,
       De la hounto d'aqueou delit ;
Et coumo l'un deis dous fau que siegue punit,
La cour dit qu'es lou Chin qu'a coumes lou dooumagi,
       L'arrest est clar coumo lou jour,
    Fouguet jugear senso appel, ni retour,
       A subir lou darnier supplici.
       Eiço, deou certo! faire hourrour ;
Mais es que troou verai : « qu'uno ounço de favour,
       Vau mai qu'un quintau de justici. »

JEAN-JOSEPH-MARIUS DIOULOUFET *(1771–1840)* *

The Tiger and The Hound

A tiger ate a stag, but claimed a hound
Was guilty of the crime. The woods around
    Resounded with the accusation;
But when the case came up for litigation,
The victim's kin, in court, produce some crows,
Witnesses to the vile abomination,
    Whose testimony clearly shows
The tiger to have wrought the deed. No matter:
    Among his friends and family
Are several judges; and, of course, the latter
Decide that such a personage as he.
Perforce, ought suffer no disgrace. And yet,
    Since someone must be guilty, let
The hound be punished for the crime committed!
And so he was. The tiger was acquitted;
The hound, condemned, despite his innocence,
    Sentenced to die!—O horrid fate!—
With no appeal, no rccourse, no defense…
Justice, it seems, though by the hundred-weight,
Weighs less than just one ounce of influence!   **

---

* Experienced francophones, probably unable fully to underftand the original, will no doubt be relieved to learn that Diouloufet wrote it, like moft of his works, not in French but in the neo-Provençal language of his native Midi. See my colleﬅion *The Fabuliﬅs French: Verse Fables of Nine Centuries* (Urbana, The University of Illinois Press, 1992), pp. 140 ff.

** This common medieval proverb is usually cited in somewhat less hyperbolic fashion, subﬅituting a *liéuro* ("pound") for the poet's *quintau: "Uno ounço de favour vau mai qu'un liéuro de juﬅici."*

ABBÉ A.-L. GUILLOUTET *(?–18??)*

Le vieux mâtin

Dans sa loge auprès de la porte,
Un vieux mâtin presque aveugle et sans dents,
Qu'on entrât, qu'on sortît, la nuit, le jour, n'importe,
Jappait sans cesse à tous venants.
Cesse tes cris, tes efforts impuissants,
Lui dit un chien voisin, tout ce bruit, ce désordre
Ne fait qu'étourdir les passants.
A quoi sert d'aboyer quand on ne peut pas mordre ?

ABBÉ A.-L. GUILLOUTET *(?–18??)* *

The Old Mastiff

     Set in his niche, beside the door,
An old hound, toothless, near bereft of sight,
Would do his best to bark—by day, by night—
At all who passed his way. though little more
Than mere yelps bore his trials, try though he might.
     A neighbor dog observes: "Wherefore,
Those useless efforts that but irk and bore
Messieurs?… Why bark through jaws that cannot bite?"

---

* It is possible that the somewhat shadowy author has been confused with others, *e.g.* Abbé A.-L. Guichelet and Abbé P. Philibert Guichelet. No matter. His (or whoever's) text remains eminently quotable.

Le marchand des chiens

Rien ne peut des mortels arrêter l'appétit ;
   Et, lorsque l'estomac réclame,
Tel vend son chien, son chat, tel autre son esprit ;
   De tout enfin l'on fait profit.
   Bravant et la honte et le blâme,
L'Anglais même, au besoin, vendrait jusqu'à sa femme.
   A Paris, sur les boulevards,
   Vous rencontrez, de toutes parts,
   Chiens de salon et chiens de chasse.
    Trente francs le basset !
    C'est un prix fait,
   Pourvu qu'il soit de bonne race.
  Marchand de chiens jamais ne vous surfait.
Chez un de ces messieurs, une chienne admirable,
   Tout à la fois par sa beauté
   Et sa rare fécondité,
   De son maître assurait la table.
Elle lui procurait douze chiens tous les ans…
   Cela faisait, en bonne arithmétique,
   Juste trois cent soixante francs.
Diane, en un pays de saine politique,
   Dans la romaine république,

BARON GOSWIN-JOSEPH-AUGUSTIN DE
   STASSART *(1780–1854)*

The Dog-Merchant *

Nothing can quell Man's lusty appetite.
    Thus when the stomach calls, some find
It meet to sell their dogs, their cats, or might   **
No less sell the creations of their mind.
    Profit is all. One knows no shame.
Whatever be the product sold, no blame…
(Need be, the Englishman will sell his wife!)
    In Paris—here, there, near and far—
    The avenues and *boulevards*
Display fine canine flesh under the knife—
All breeds: lap-dogs, curs, hunting dogs… The lot!
And the dog-butcher never asks for more
Than what each beast ought well be purchased for:
    Bassets may fetch twelve francs, much sought!
        Gone in a trice
        At such a price!…
Well, one of these fine merchants owned a bitch
Of beauty rare and rare fecundity
As well—especially the latter, which
Filled full her master's bill-of-fare, as she
Provided him a dozen pups per year…

---

* I apologize to dog-lovers, like myself, for deciding to translate this rather unpleasant fable. But in the interest of variety, I present it.

** Obviously, my pun does not occur in the original.

Aurait été, je crois, exempte de l'impôt
Notre spéculateur n'y voyait pas si haut.
   Loin de nourrir la pauvre mère,
   A sa faim loin de satisfaire,
   Chaque jour il imaginait,
  De retrancher quelque chose au potage
   Que vers le soir on lui portait.
  Elle gémit, se plaint, se décourage…
   La faim, la douleur et la rage
   La conduisirent chez Pluton.

   M'entendez-vous, suppôts de la finance ?
Ma fable vous présente une sage leçon !
   Pour nous conserver l'abondance,
Renoncez quelquefois à la fiscalité :
   Garantir au peuple la vie,
   En ménageant son industrie,
   Peut avoir son utilité.

By my arithmetic, his profit came
To some hundred and sixty francs—no mere
Pittance—that might have spared Diane (her name)
From paying tax, were she a citizen
Of Rome, or other state republican!
Not for our merchant though! He soon began—
Despite his handsome profit from her passions!
Greedy purveyor, he!—to cut her rations—
    Till, though she whine, bark, and complain,
Her hunger, anger, and her belly's pain,
    In time, will do the poor bitch in,
And whisk her off to Pluto's dark domain…

Do you hear, O beast-butcher kith and kin?
My fable's message is one you ought heed!
Would you preserve abundance? You should, then,
Ignore—at times, at least—the vice of greed.
    Demand no more of workingmen
    Than they can give, or than they would.
More "less" than "more" may serve the public good.

LE BARON GOSWIN-JOSEPH-AUGUSTIN DE
   STASSART *(1780–1854)*

Les enfants, l'épagneul et le bouledogue

A l'ombre d'un saule pleureur,
Sur le gazon, non loin de la fontaine,
Louis et sa plus jeune sœur
D'un déjeuner friand savouraient la douceur.
Tout autour d'eux, pour partager l'aubaine,
Un charmant épagneul s'agite et se promène ;
Il sollicite un os qu'il ne peut obtenir…
C'est en vain qu'il se met en frais de gentillesse.
Hélas ! Pas la moindre largesse !
On lui laisse sa faim, dût-il même en mourir.
Arrive un bouledogue, à la voix formidable…
Il se fait écouter de nos petits marmots ;
On le craint, il reçoit un accueil très aimable ;
On lui prodigue les morceaux.

On ménage les gens, selon qu'on les redoute.
Maint député, qui nous écoute,
Sait que cette maxime a chez nos gouvernants,
Force de loi ; bien plus que les talents,
Des honneurs elle ouvre la route.

BARON GOSWIN-JOSEPH-AUGUSTIN DE STASSART
  (1780–1854)

The Children, the Spaniel, and the Bulldog

In weeping willow's shade, beside a brook,
A lad—Louis—and his young sister took
    Their meal: a tasty *déjeuner*
Sur l'herbe… A spaniel frisks about as they
Savor each morsel… Dog hopes he may be
Lucky enough—in their propinquity—
To share, perhaps, a bit of their largesse.
    He begs a bone. A "nay" is what
He gets! Sweet, loving pet, his graciousness
And loving nature win him nothing but
    The chance to starve before the pair
    Of thoughtless scamps, for all they care!
But then, arrives a bulldog on the scene—
Fierce air ferocious, manner passing mean!—
The two, agape, give ear. They hear him, heed him,
And, shuddering with fear, are quick to feed him!

Fear is the force that dictates how we will
    Treat others. Those who govern us
Know that this maxim rules the day. And, thus,
    More than our talents or our skill,
Opens the way to honors glorious!

J.-J.-ILDEPHONSE GUIEU *(18??–18??)*

Le chien coupable

Pourquoi Médor est-il inquiet, soucieux,
Lui si folâtre et si gai d'ordinaire ?
   On dirait que sur toi, mon père,
   Il n'ose plus lever les yeux.
   —C'est que Médor se sent coupable ;
   Il vient de voler un chapon,
      Et maintenant le fripon
   Craint que de coups je ne l'accable.

Devant qui que ce soit, en tout temps, en tous lieux,
   Veux-tu porter la tête haute ?
   Mon fils, ne commets point de faute
   Qui t'oblige à baisser les yeux.

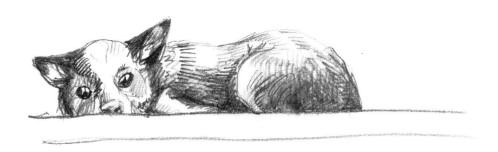

J.-J.-ILDEPHONSE GUIEU *(18??–18??)*

The Guilty Dog

"Why, father, is Médor so troubled? He *
Who always plays and frisks so gaily? Why,
  He scarcely dares to raise an eye
  And look at you, pathetically."
"What you see is the guilt Médor is feeling.
  He stole a capon, little thief!
  And he fears lest he come to grief
  Beneath the blows I may be dealing!"

If you, my son, in every circumstance,
  Would stand with head held high, then, pray,
  Commit no crime or sin that may
Cause you, in shame, to cast a downward glance.

---

* Médor has long been a traditional French name for a dog, possibly stemming from the name of a Saracen hero in Ariosto's *Orlando furioso* of 1516.

J.-J.-ILDEPHONSE GUIEU *(18??–18??)*

Do et le chien malade

En rongeant un os que son maître
Venait de lui donner
Pour son dîner,
Tout près de lui Do vit paraître
Un vieux mâtin gras comme un cent de clous,
Et recevant moins de pain que de coups.
Le pauvre diable était malade,
Abandonné du médecin,
D'une lieue à la ronde il sentait le sapin
Et n'avait pas un camarade
Qui voulût lui donner le plus mince lopin.
Ce malheureux qu'on chasse et qu'on repousse
Serre le cœur de Do, qui l'appelle et soudain
Lui dit de sa voix la plus douce :
Tiens, mange, mon ami, va, moi je n'ai pas faim.

J.-J.-ILDEPHONSE GUIEU *(18??–18??)*

Do and the Sick Dog

A dog named Do sits gnawing on a bone—
    One that his master gave him—when,
        Just then,
    He sees appear, old and alone,
    Interrupting his meager dinner,
A scrawny mastiff, skin and bones, far thinner
Even than the proverbial "hundred nails,"   *
    Fed more on beatings than on bread...
Doctors have not the slightest guess what ails
    The poor sick creature, well nigh dead,
      Who, with his every breath,
    Seems to spread round the smell of death,
With never a friend to offer him a crumb!
Do's heart breaks at the sorry sight. "Friend, come,
Help me! I cannot take another bite.
Finish my meal... I have no appetite."

---

* The ironic French expression *"gras comme un cent de clous"* (fat as a hundred nails), less common today than in generations paſt, has occasionally found its way into English literature as "thin as a hundred nails." The logic behind it appears to be that, if one nail is thin, a hundred are much more so.

CLAUDE-THÉOPHILE DUCHAPT *(1802–1858)*

Le chien qui jappe après la lune

Un chien toutes les nuits jappait après la lune.
  Un des bœufs qu'il allait gardant,
Las à la fin d'ouïr ce concert discordant,
Lui dit : « Fais trêve aux cris dont ta gueule importune
  Nous étourdit incessamment.
  A l'astre, objet de ta rancune,
  Pour insulter utilement,
  Attends qu'il tombe ou qu'il descende ;
  Car, si haut qu'il est, franchement,
  Je ne suis pas sûr qu'il t'entende. »

CLAUDE-THÉOPHILE DUCHAPT *(1802–1858)*

The Hound Who Bays at the Moon

A yelping hound, each night, bays at the moon.
    An ox entrusted to his care,
One of the herd, balks at his bark and blare—
Discordant concert!—pleading: "Cur, a boon!
    Pray, cease that din cacophonous
    That deafens, irks, and nettles us!
    As for the moon, who galls you so,
Wiser were you to vent more useful wrath!
Best wait until he falls, or beats a path
    From high above to here below,
    Whence he might even settle near you…
Frankly, up there, I fear he scarce can hear you!"   *

---

* Readers will appreciate the frequency of this subject. See, for example, the more detailed example by Nicolas Grozelier (p. 36).

VICTOR HUGO *(1802–1885)*

La mort d'un chien

Un groupe tout à l'heure était là sur la grève,
Regardant quelque chose à terre. —Un chien qui crève !
M'ont crié des enfants ; voilà tout ce que c'est.—
Et j'ai vu sous leurs pieds un vieux chien qui gisait.
L'océan lui jetait l'écume de ses lames.
—Voilà trois jours qu'il est ainsi, disaient des femmes,
On a beau lui parler, il n'ouvre pas les yeux.
—Son maître est un marin absent, disait un vieux.
Un pilote, passant la tête à sa fenêtre,
A repris : —Ce chien meurt de ne plus voir son maître.
Justement le bateau vient d'entrer dans le port ;
Le maître va venir, mais le chien sera mort.—
Je me suis arrêté près de la triste bête,
Qui, sourde, ne bougeant ni le corps ni la tête,
Les yeux fermés, semblait morte sur le pavé.
Comme le soir tombait, le maître est arrivé,
Vieux lui-même ; et, hâtant son pas que l'âge casse,
A murmuré le nom de son chien à voix basse.
Alors, rouvrant ses yeux pleins d'ombre, exténué,
Le chien a regardé son maître, a remué
Une dernière fois sa pauvre vieille queue,
Puis est mort. C'était l'heure où, sous la voûte bleue,
Comme un flambeau qui sort d'un gouffre, Vénus luit ;
Et j'ai dit : D'où vient l'astre ? où va le chien ? ô nuit !

VICTOR HUGO *(1802–1885)*

Death of a Dog

A group on shore peers down at something lying
Sprawled on the sand. "It's nothing but a dying
Dog!" cry some urchins. "Nothing more…" My gaze
Lights on the tide that spits its frothy haze
About an old hound at their feet. "He's there
For three whole days now, just like that," declare
Some womenfolk. "Though everybody tries
To rouse him, he scarce opens up his eyes!"
An old salt pipes: "His master went to sea…"
And, leaning out a window, earnestly,
A skipper adds: "Poor thing! His every breath—
Without his master—drags him to his death…
But look! His boat, I think…" And someone said:
"Too late… His master comes, but he'll be dead!…"
I stood next to the silent beast, who lay,
Eyes shut, head, body still—who, one would say,
Seemed dead already… Night… His master came,
Stumbling, age-bent as well… Sighed the dog's name…
The dog flickers his gloom-enshrouded eyes,
Wags, one last time, his tired old tail… And dies.
I muse, that moment when sky's arching hue
Spreads over earth its span of darkening blue,
And depth-born Venus, torch-like, rises bright:
"Whence comes that star? Whither that dog?… O night!"

PIERRE LACHAMBEAUDIE *(1806–1872)*

Le poulet, le renard et le chien

« Petit ! Petit ! Petit ! disait maître renard
A certain beau poulet qu'il couvait du regard.
     Approche, ami que je t'embrasse… »
Cette voix hypocrite et cet œil caressant,
Hélas ! Vont à sa perte attirer l'innocent.
     Mylord, un chien de race,
     Apparaît menaçant,
     Ouvre une gueule redoutable ;
     D'un hurlement épouvantable
Il chasse le renard qui court et court encor,
Et le poulet se sauve, en maudissant Mylord.
Le flatteur, on l'a vu, ne rêvait que carnage,
     Et le grondeur fut bienfaisant :
     Il vaut mieux le bâton du sage
     Que le baiser du courtisan.

PIERRE LACHAMBEAUDIE *(1806–1872)*

The Chicken, the Fox, and the Hound

"Come, come, my pretty! Eat your feed..." So did
Master Fox, wheedling, cry as he would bid
A tempting chicken he was ogling with
Covetous eyes. "Come eat, and let me kiss
Your loveliness!" True to his kin and kith,
Our hypocrite, with foxly artifice,
Would have succeeded and—alas, alack!—
Done in the victim of his tongue's attack,
Were it not for a hound of pedigree—
    Mylord, by name—who, presently
    Appears, opens his fearsome jaws,
Growls a fierce growl! At which—no hems, no haws—
Off flees Fox... Running yet, I guarantee!   *
Chicken curses Mylord for "meddling" in
His life, unmindful that he saved his skin!
    Better the wise man's cudgel than
The kiss of hypocritic courtesan.

---

* Devotees of iconic fabulist La Fontaine will doubtless hear in the original line's *"et court encore"* an echo of the last line of his equally dramatic "Le Loup et le Chien" (I, 5): *"Cela dit, maître Loup s'enfuit, et court encor."* For an English translation see my volume *The Complete Fables of Jean de La Fontaine* (Urbana, University of Illinois Press, 2007, pp. 7, 8).

Le chien et le lion

Sous un sceptre de fer courbant les animaux,
Le lion, roi cruel, les accablait de maux ;
Comme les dieux païens il vivait d'hécatombes.
Chacun a ses tyrans : les cerfs et les colombes
Dans l'air et dans les bois périssent tous les jours
Sous l'angle des lions, sous le bec des vautours.
Tous pleuraient sous le poids d'un pénible esclavage,
Lorsqu'un chien se dévoue, et, s'armant de courage,
Pour le salut commun gagne l'antre du roi.
Voulant frapper son cœur d'un salutaire effroi,
« Apprenez, lui dit-il, qu'un cri de délivrance,
Peut remplacer bientôt le cri de la souffrance,
Et que le ciel, témoin de nos affreux tourments,
Vous réserve la foudre et de longs châtiments.
Vous verrez dans vos nuits chaque pâle victime
Troubler votre sommeil et vous glacer d'horreur.
Allons, quittez enfin le noir sentier du crime… »
Le lion, à ces mots, étrangla l'orateur.

Plus d'un noble avocat d'une cause sublime,
Pour ses frères bravant la colère des rois,
Gémit dans les cachots ou mourut sur la croix !

PIERRE LACHAMBEAUDIE *(1806–1872)*

The Dog and the Lion

With iron scepter, heartless potentate,
King Lion held his subjects in a state
Of subjugation. Like the gods of old—
The pagan panoply—murders untold
Defined his bloody reign. Each beast would fall
Prey to its tyrant: birds, animals all—
Dove, deer, the lot!—a feckless slave was kept
To great cat's claw, to vulture's beak! All wept
Their servile fate… Until a dog, one day,
Would selflessly decide that he would lay
Their case before him… To his den he goes,
Reckless, and to the king decries their woes,
Hoping he might, with fright, discourage thus
The cruel excesses of his barbarous
Regime… "Mercy! Let sighs of peace, great king,
Redeem the cries of dark crime's suffering,
Lest heaven heap full your sleep with torments! Lest
You dream each haggard victim's horror, best
Mend your ways!" Lion, loath to listen more,
Forthwith strangles his interlocutor.

Such, too, those noble champions, who—times past—
Would save their kind from monarch's clutches fell,
But died upon the cross, or gasped their last,
With mournful moan, cast in death's dungeon cell.

AUGUSTE FISCH *(1814–1881)*

La vengeance d'un caniche

Un jour je vis passer, étant à la fenêtre,
Un pauvre chien d'aveugle ; il conduisait son maître,
Et marchait gravement penché sur son collier,
Comme un brave animal qui sait bien son métier.
Chacun en le voyant disait : la bonne bête !
Comme avec conscience elle fait son devoir,
Comme elle tire bien ! C'est plaisir de la voir
Trotter sans détourner un seul moment la tête !
Tout à coup j'entendis un sourd gémissement ;
Qu'est ceci ? M'écriai-je… Avec étonnement
J'aperçus le vieillard frappant avec colère
De son bâton noueux l'animal débonnaire ;
Son crime était de s'être un instant oublié,
Et pour ce seul motif il frappait sans pitié.
Et je dis à part moi : l'ingrat, le misérable !
Battre un chien si fidèle, oh ! C'est abominable !
Pour moi, si j'étais chien, sur un maître si dur
Je sauterais bien vite, et le mordrais pour sûr !
Bravo ! Je suis content ! … Le voilà qui s'élance,
Le mord… Il le lécha ! Ce fut là sa vengeance !

AUGUSTE FISCH *(1814–1881)*

A Poodle's Revenge

Standing one day before my window, I
Watched as a guide-dog led a blind man by.   *
The noble beast trod ploddingly, head bent,
His eyes scanning the master's path, intent
On serving him. All those who saw him said:
"Oh, the fine animal! See how he knows
His task, how conscientiously he goes
Straight, undeterred, without turning his head!
A joy to see!... But suddenly I heard
A low whine, as the blind man flailed and stirred
This way and that, stout stick in hand. What's this?
Something, I fear, is very much amiss,
As, angrily, he whips his gentle guide,
Whose crime was that, one moment, cloudy-eyed,
He erred a bit... Oh, woe and welladay!
Ingrate! To flout a faithful dog that way!
Were I a dog, with such a heartless master,
You may be sure, I would pounce on him faster
Than fast, repay him with a bite or two!...
Ah, look!... Bravo!... He does what I would do...
Leaps... Bites... But no! What?... Licks his hand!... Ah yes,
A dog's sweetest revenge? His tenderness!

---

* One might have expected the guide-dog here to be a German shepherd or other tra-
ditional breeds. Actually, the poodle makes a superb service-dog thanks to its excep-
tional intelligence and desire to please its master.

Le chien et le flacon

« —Mon beau chien, mon bon chien, mon cher toutou, approchez et venez respirer un excellent parfum acheté chez le meilleur parfumeur de la ville. » Et le chien, en frétillant de la queue, ce qui est, je crois, chez ces pauvres êtres, le signe correspondant du rire et du sourire, s'approche et pose curieusement son nez humide sur le flacon débouché ; puis, reculant soudainement avec effroi, il aboie contre moi, en manière de reproche.

« —Ah ! misérable chien, si je vous avais offert un paquet d'excréments, vous l'auriez flairé avec délices et peut-être dévoré. Ainsi, vous-même, indigne compagnon de ma triste vie, vous ressemblez au public, à qui il ne faut jamais présenter des parfums délicats qui l'exaspèrent, mais des ordures soigneusement choisies. »

CHARLES BAUDELAIRE *(1821–1867)*

The Dog and the Perfume Vial   *

"My fine dog, my good dog, my dear little pup… Come here and smell this excellent perfume bought from the city's most outstanding perfumer." And the dog, wagging his tail—which, among these poor creatures, corresponds, I think, to a laugh or a smile—comes over and, with a quizzical look, presses his moist snout against the un-stoppered vial, only to pull away suddenly, in fright, and give a bark as if to scold me.

"Ah, miserable cur! If I had offered you a packet of dung, you would have sniffed it with delight, and perhaps even gobbled it down! You, worthless companion of my sad existence! How much like the public you are… The public, whom we should never present with delicate perfumes, which quite distress them, but only with all manner of swill, selected with the utmost care!"

---

* Practitioner of the seemingly oxymoronic *poème en prose*, of which the present is a superb example, Baudelaire needs no aesthetic defense. I do, however, resist the temptation of including his majestic, multi-page opus, "The Good Dogs," which rather exceeds the bounds for this collection—really more an essay than a prose poem.

Le chien malade

        Un chien de célèbre origine,
Bien nourri, bien luisant, gras et de haute mine.
Sur un tapis soyeux mollement étendu,
Semblait, à son air triste, à son regard perdu,
Porter péniblement le fardeau de la vie :
Il geignait, aucun mets n'excitait son envie.
Aussitôt grand émoi dans toute la maison :
        « Qu'a donc Azor ? se disait-on ;
        Lui qui fait toujours table nette,
        Lui d'ordinaire si gourmet,
        Voilà qu'il détourne la tête
        Devant une aile de poulet !
Azor, l'amour des chiens, et qui jamais ne gronde,
        Semble en vouloir à tout le monde !
D'un pareil changement quelle est donc la raison ? … »
Le pauvre Azor avait une indigestion.

C'est ainsi que se fait l'opinion des hommes ;
Ainsi nous résonnons, et tous, tant que nous sommes,
Avons-nous le teint frais et le jarret dispos,
        L'appétit vient-il à propos,

ANATOLE DE SÉGUR *(1823–1902)*

The Sick Dog

A dog, well bred, of pedigree
Distinguished, boasting an old family tree—
Handsome, with shining coat, plump and well fed—
On carpet silken-soft lay spread,
Languid of glance, a faraway
Look in his eye… All night and day,
Wailing beneath life's weighty burden, quite
Un-tempted by his food, no appetite
Urging him on… The household folk, distressed,
Wonder: "What ails Azor? He, hungriest   *
Of hounds, who always licks the platter
Clean! Dog-gourmet! Whatever is the matter?
See how he turns his head, poor thing,
And spurns even a chicken-wing!
He, never known to groan or growl,
Yet seems to look on everyone a-foul!
Why? Why?…" The answer to the burning question?
Poor Azor has a case of indigestion!

So is it, too, with all of us.
We think the world's condition echoes thus
Our own. Are we firm-fleshed, in fettle fine,

---

* Perhaps less popular a French dog-name today, than in earlier generations, Azor, an Old Testament name meaning "helper," remains in the canine catalogue, and is even found in several other languages. It was, in fact, the name of George Washington's pet greyhound.

Les choses sont au mieux, vive la république !
Chacun se faisant en deux mots
Ce raisonnement sans réplique :
« Tout va bien, puisque je vais bien,
Et lorsque j'ai dîné, nul n'a besoin de rien. »
Mais qu'il survienne un mal, un rhume, une colique,
Nous tournons à la philippique ;
Le peuple est une dupe et l'État un vaurien,
Il faut désespérer de la chose publique.

Hardy of limb and fair, pink-fresh of cheek?
Do we relish our hearty food and wine?
Then all is well! *Vive la République!*
Do we say: "Since I eat my fill, how could
Anyone not eat all he will?…" But, should
Discomfort strike—a cold, a belly-ache—
 Oh, what a solemn fuss we make!
 The people? Dupes! The government?
 On the State's dissolution bent!
  All worthless "so-and-sos"!
  And so it goes…

VALÉRY DERBIGNY *(mid–19th century)*

La querelle des chiens

Deux chiens, d'humeur assez cruelle,
Pour un os à ronger, s'étaient pris de querelle,
Ils se disputaient au plus fort,
Et dans leur ardeur meurtrière,
Ils allaient s'échiner de la belle manière,
Quand un autre survient qui veut mettre l'accord.
Sans doute à l'endroit du tapage
Il fut conduit par un funeste sort ;
Nos querelleurs avides de carnage,
Fâchés qu'on vînt s'enquérir de leur tort,
Sur le médiateur assouvirent leur rage
Et l'étranglèrent tout d'abord.

La Fontaine ou Deshoulières
Nous l'a dit en quelque endroit :
Ne mettons jamais le doigt
Entre deux mâchelières.

VALÉRY DERBIGNY *(mid–19th century)*

The Hounds' Quarrel

A pair of hounds, belligerent,
Of vicious air, each found a bone,
Fit to be gnawed. On combat bent,
Each one, intent to make the prize his own,
They fall to snarl and snort, and thus
Would soon have rent, with ardor murderous,
Each one the other, limb from limb,
Had not a third—whom their howled growls attracted,
Drawn by a deadly fate—reacted,
Come to make peace… Alack! Woe unto him!
Our brawlers yearn for blood… Foe-fashion, pounce…
Turn on the mediator… Trounce
And strangle him, to satisfy
Their passion, then and there, thereby.

La Fontaine or La Deshoulières   *
(Which one? No matter!) says somewhere:
"Lest your hand feel the bite of pain,
Best place it not 'twixt molars twain!"

---

* Neither poet appears to have used the specific quotation. Symbolically, for La Fontaine, one thinks immediately of his fable on the dangers of mediating between two enemies, "The Vultures and the Pigeons" (VII, 7), that advises, not nearly as picturesquely as the more graphic Derbigny: "So? Would you live a peaceful life? / Then keep your enemies at war! / A passing thought… I'll say no more." See my *The Complete Fables of Jean de La Fontaine,* Urbana, University of Illinois Press, 2007, pp. 166-68. For Antoinette Deshoulières (1638–1694) obviously paired here with him for the rhyme, I can't say which, if any, of her typically short forms Derbigny may have had in mind.

L'Automobile

Sur les coussins capitonnés
D'une voiture automobile,
Le caniche Médor, digne, fier, immobile,
Trônait, les lunettes au nez.
La vitesse était sa marotte.
Pataud, pauvre chien qui trotte
Dans la crotte,
Dont les ébats par l'auto sont gênés,
Jappe à Médor ses abois indignés :
« Quel plaisir trouves-tu sur cette mécanique,
Qui répand partout la panique ?
Est-ce digne d'un chien ? N'as-tu pas de remords
En songeant que, pour te distraire,
Tu risques d'écraser un frère ?
Combien de nous déjà par les autos sont morts !
Crois-moi, descends ; notre mère Nature
Nous a donné des pattes pour marcher.
Quatre pattes ! quand l'homme, infirme créature,
N'en a que deux ! C'est pour cacher
Cette infirmité de structure
Qu'il prit le cheval pour monture,
Qu'il se fit chauffeur ou cocher.
Tout n'est en lui que ruse et qu'imposture,
Dur égoïsme ou vanité.
Nous avons trop longtemps subi sa dictature.
Il nous faut affranchir d'un engin redouté
Par sa malice inventé.

EMILE COUTEAU *(1837–1931)*

The Automobile

Astride his cushions, puffed with pride,
Médor the poodle sits, genteel,   *
Delighting in the swift automobile
That speeds him through the countryside,
Begoggled, poised, and oh so dignified.
Another pup—mongrel Pataud— trotting among
The muck and dung,
Distraught, unable to abide
Having his canine playground occupied
By the mechanical invader,
Barks at Médor: "For shame, my fancy promenader!
Is that what proper dogs should do?
You go cavorting on that metal giant,
Spreading his panic—cynical, defiant—
Trampling on fellow creatures just like you!
How many a brother dog lies lifeless in the street?
Alas, I fear not just a few!...
Come now, Nature knew best. She gave us feet
To walk with... All four paws... A set... Complete...
Unlike mere Man, with but this paltry two!
(It was, in fact—and *entre nous*—
To hide his structural deficiency
And make up for the two he lacked, that he
Saddled and reined the horse, poor servant tried and true.)

---

* See p. 85, note. Médor's mutt antagonist, Pataud, whose name was sarcastically chosen, recalls vociferous leftist labor leader Emile Pataud, champion of the working class and obdurate unionist.

Quoique tu sois un chien de qualité,
        Viens avec nous, chiens de roture ;
J'en appelle à ton cœur honnête et délicat.
        Nous formerons un syndicat
Pour empêcher qu'aucun auto ne s'aventure
Sur tous chemins par nous, libres chiens, fréquentés !
        Ainsi le veut l'égalité,
Ainsi s'établira pour la race future
Le règne du progrès et de la liberté ! »

« Je craindrais, » dit Médor, « une mésavanture
        Si j'écoutais votre ressentiment.
Selon qu'on est en bonne ou mauvaise posture,
        On voit les choses autrement.
        Vous parleriez, je crois, différemment,
        Si vous étiez dans la voiture. »

Médor avait raison de n'être pas la dupe
        Des plaintes de son concurrent.
        Tout prend un aspect différent
        Suivant la place qu'on occupe.

Man, that self-centered master who,
By wile and ruse and treachery
Has ruled too long! Dog's day is overdue!
Rise up! Down with the auto! Help us free
Our streets from fear. Forget your pedigree,
Aristocratic through and through.
Come, join our cause, commoners though we be.
We'll form a union and we'll rout the enemy.
Be true and stout of heart. It's time we overthrew
Man the oppressor; time that we
Stood up to him and struck a coup
For progress, dogdom… and for liberty!"
Médor replied: "Your dire complaints unending
Strike me as so much ballyhoo.
Truth is, we find things fair or foul, depending
Simply upon our point of view.
I fear your attitude would be far less unbending
Were you, my friend, here in the auto too."
Médor was right. It's only fitting
Not to be fooled by such invective.
Opinion is a matter of perspective:
It all depends on where you're sitting.

ANDRÉ GILL *(1840–1885)* et
LOUIS DE GRAMONT *(1854–1912)*

La levrette et le gamin
(Histoire parisienne)

Écoutez l'histoir' du gamin,
Du gamin et de la levrette !
L'un demeurait à la Villette ;
L'autre habitait faubourg Germain !

C'était une levrette exquise ;
Je n' sais plus comme elle s'app'lait ;
Mais c'était la chienn' d'un' marquise,
Qui de la levrett' raffolait.
C'te p'tit' bête était adorée,
Tell'ment qu'aux Tuil'ri's, chaque jour,
On l'envoyait faire un p'tit tour
Avec un larbin en livrée !

Quant au gamin, c'était l' gavroche
Qui parcourt Paris en tous sens,
Et qui, sans peur et sans reproche,

ANDRÉ GILL *(1840–1885)* and
LOUIS DE GRAMONT *(1854–1912)*

The Little Greyhound Bitch and the Urchin
(A Parisian tale)

I'd like to tell a tale in which
A lad from La Villette nonplussed
A high-brow little greyhound bitch
From Saint-Germain's rich uppercrust.   *

Peerless, her bitchly qualities!
(Sorry, her name's escaping me.)
For she belonged to a *marquise,*
Who loved the houndlet utterly,
Worshiped, adored her; and, indeed,
Every day sent her promenading,
Tuileries-bound, proudly parading
Round, with groom lushly liveried.

The urchin—typical Gavroche,
Well known under the Paris sky—
Young scamp, "sans peur et sans reproche"—   **

---

* La Villette and Saint-Germain were then, as now, Parisian *quartiers* at the opposite extremes of the social scale.

** Readers will recognize Victor Hugo's homeless, street-smart gamin of his 1862 novel *Les Misérables,* whose name, in French, has become a common noun. If not from the novel, they may know it from the recent musical adaptations—French, 1980, English, 1985—or the subsequent film adaptations. They are less likely to recognize the reference to the heroic Chevalier de Bayard (1473–1524), admiringly known throughout history as *"le chevalier sans peur et sans reproche"* (the fearless knight beyond reproach), an epithet used for our urchin with tongue clearly in cheek.

Flân', rigole et blagu' les passants,
Or, un jour qu'aux Tuil'ri's (mazette !
Ça se cors' comm' du Montépin !)
Il était planté d'vant l' bassin,
Précisément pass' la levrette…

Contre le goss' levant la patte,
La levrett',—cett' chienn' de salon,—
Avec un' morgu' d'aristocrate
Lui compiss' tout son pantalon.
Le gamin sent l' pipi qui l' mouille,
I' s' retourne, i fait du potin…
Mais de la levrett' le larbin
Le trait' de p'tit' gouape et d' fripouille !

L'gamin, jurant de s' venger, file
La bête et l' laquais sans êt' vu…
Jusqu'à leur noble domicile
Il les suit d' loin, à leur insu…
Su' l' pas d' la porte, au bout d'une heure,
La p'tit' levrett' vient prendre l'air…
L' gamin l'empoign', prompt comm' l'éclair,
Et l'entraîn' loin de sa demeure !

Il lui fit faire, à la Villette,
Connaissanc' d'un caniche affreux…
La levrette agit en levrette !
Ell' prit l' canich' pour amoureux.
Deux jours plus tard dans la soirée,

Just sits and twits the passers-by…
Now, in the Tuileries one day
(Readers of Montépin take note:
His tales dwell on such anecdote),   ***
Bitch and her lackey come his way.

Joining the lad—before, beside,
Behind—our most aristocratic
Salon-bred bitch, with grimace snide,
Pees, with slick gesture acrobatic,   ****
Soaking his trouser-legs; whereat
The urchin, drenched and angry—very!—
Stinking of her feat urinary,
Howls: "Piss!…" Flunkey cries: "Foul-mouthed brat!"

Said brat, vowing revenge, takes care
To track them on their homeward road,
Keeping his distance as the pair—
Groom and bitch—reach their rich abode…
After an hour or so, the latter,
Eager to get some air, steps out…
Quick as a flash, our urchin lout
Kidnaps—no, "*bitch*naps" her. (No matter!)

In La Villette he introduces
Her to a mangy poodle mutt.
She yields to his fleshly abuses,

*** Xavier de Montépin (1823–1902) was a prolific and successful author of serial novels characterized by their sensational and sentimental plots and popular characters.

**** The original says that she raises her leg to pee. Certain that the poets knew the difference between male and female dogs' anatomies, I take the liberty of attributing to our bitch a physical skill necessary to perform her feat.

Lâchée enfin par le gamin,
Ell' reparut faubourg Germain…
Mais elle était déshonorée !

Peu d'temps après, ell' mit au monde,
Non sans quelques douleurs de reins,
Six cabots d'un' laideur immonde,
Bâtards, p't'-êt' même adultérins !...
Mais l' plus bath de l'historiette
C'est qu' la marquis', tout récemment,
A pris son cocher pour amant,
Histoir' d'imiter la levrette !

Et voilà l'histoir' du gamin,
Du gamin et de la levrette !
Quel triomphe pour la Villette !
Quel deuil pour le faubourg Germain !

Taking him for her lover… But,
Once freed, to Saint-Germain she trots,
Where, in a trice, one finds—surprised?—
That she's been roundly compromised!
The price for having got the hots!

Soon she gives birth: half-dozen curs.
Though long-drawn is the pain, and bitter,
Worst of all are those pups of hers—
This ugly, six-mutt bastard litter!
But that's not all. The best is that
Madame *marquise*, love's itch in bloom,
Makes like her bitch! With whom? The groom!
Madame… That fine aristocrat!

So ends the tale I tell, in which
A lad from La Villette nonplussed
A high-brow little greyhound bitch!
Cheers in Villette!… Germain? Disgust!

A. DE BLANCHE *(????–????)*

Le chien qu'on noie

Pourquoi noyer ce chien ? —C'est que toujours il grogne.
    —Si l'on noyait tous les hargneux,
    Les hommes seraient moins nombreux.
Pourquoi tuer ton chien ? —Eh ! C'est qu'il a la rogne.
    —Si l'on tuait tous les rogneux,
    Les hommes seraient moins nombreux.
Sous tes coups assommé le pauvre animal râle,
    Sa douceur ne lui sert de rien ;
    A-t-il décidément la gale ?
    —La gale et mieux, homme de bien,
    Il est hydrophobe. —Fort bien,
    Je m'attendais à ce langage :
Le proverbe le dit : veut-on tuer son chien,
    On affirme qu'il a la rage.

A. DE BLANCHE *(???? –????)*

The Dog One Would Drown   *

"Why drown that dog?" "He whines and howls."
"If we drowned every howler, we
Would lose much of humanity!
Why kill your dog?" "He gnarls and growls."
"If we killed every growler, we
Would lose much of humanity!
Does he snarl, friend, because you beat him?
Poor, gentle beast, do you mistreat him?
Or is it mange, scabies, and such?
"Scabies? Mange? Far worse, forasmuch!…
He fears the water… See his frothing jaws!"
"I might have guessed you would claim such the cause!
The proverb tells those who would be
Rid of their dog: 'If you your dog would kill,
Say he has rabies! Others will
Dispatch him for you blamelessly.'"

---

* For the sake of variety, and so as not to deny this virtually unknown versifier his modest place in the sun, I include the present rather free version of a subject we have seen treated by a far more prolific and talented poet. See Boisard, p. 49, and the note to that poem regarding the ancient proverb in question.

MAURICE ROLLINAT *(1846–1903)*

Le chien enragé

Le chien noir me poursuit dans l'orage
A travers de hideux pays plats,
Et tous deux, tristes comme des glas,
Nous passons labour et pâturage.

Il franchit buisson, mur et barrage…
Et je n'ai pas même un échalas !
Le chien noir me poursuit dans l'orage
A travers de hideux pays plats.

Et, songeant aux martyrs de la rage
Qu'on étouffe entre deux matelas,
Je chemine, effroyablement las,
Presqu'à bout de force et de courage…
Le chien noir me poursuit dans l'orage !

MAURICE ROLLINAT *(1846–1903)*

The Mad Dog

The black dog, through the storm, comes chasing me   *
Over plains reeking of a hideous hell,
And both of us, sad as bells' mourning-knell,
Trample pasture and harvest, cap-a-pie.

He leaps bush, wall, and dam, unyieldingly…
I have nor stick nor cudgel, truth to tell!
The black dog, through the storm comes chasing me
Over plains reeking of a hideous hell.

And musing on mad martyrs who would be
Strangled a-bed, choked to a fare-thee-well,
I flee, alarmingly undone, pell-mell,
Feeling my strength wane, and my bravery…
The black dog, through the storm, comes chasing me!

---

* Nine-syllable lines being not particularly effective in English, I resist using them in this poem typical of Rollinat's "dark" inspiration, to which he owes much of his popularity.

MAURICE ROLLINAT *(1846–1903)*

Mort de pistolet

Mon fidèle partout, sûr en toute saison,
Par qui je ruminais des chimères meilleures,
Ma vraie âme damnée, humble à toutes les heures,
Mon ami des chemins comme de la maison.

Mon veilleur qui, pour moi, faisait guetter son somme,
Qui, par sa tendre humeur, engourdissait mon mal,
M'offrant sans cesse, au lieu du renfermé de l'homme,
Dans ses bons yeux parlants, son âme d'animal.

Il repose à jamais là, mangé par la terre,
Mais je l'ai tant aimé, d'un cœur si solitaire,
Que tout son cher aspect, tel qu'il fut, me revient.

L'appel de mon regret met toujours à mes trousses,
Retrottinant, câlin sous ses couleurs bruns-rousses,
Le fantôme béni de mon pauvre vieux chien.

MAURICE ROLLINAT *(1846–1903)*

Pistolet's Death

Faithful companion, creature true and tried,
Source of my best chimera-dreams... Meek, hell-
Damned soul, this other "me", hell-damned as well:
Hearth-mate, road-partner, ever by my side...

My guard, wakeful lest he, in sleep, might be
Caught short... Who tried to numb my pain, whose eyes
Spoke more than dumb-tongued Man, and offered me
His soul: animal gaze in human guise...

See, there he lies, forever earth-consumed.
Oh, how I loved him! Now, alone and doomed
To woe, I call... And lo! Here, bounding yet—

Before, behind—trotting his ups and downs,
Nuzzling me, clad in russet reds and browns:
The blessèd phantom of my poor old pet...

HENRY MACQUERON *(1853–1937)*

Le chien vertueux

Deux chiens s'amusaient peu, laissés seuls au logis.
L'un d'eux, pour se distraire inspectant la cuisine,
Se prit à méditer sur des restes farcis.
Le vol est assez laid, laide aussi la famine :
Le fouet a des rigueurs ou plus tard en aura ;
　　　　Bah ! Plus tard on s'avisera ;
　　　　Et la viande a si bonne mine !
　　　Enfin tout vu, tout pesé, le reclus
　　　　　　Tombe dessus.
La besogne allait bien, lorsque le camarade,
　　　　Qui promenait son air maussade,
Vient lui faire un discours plein de moralité.
　　　　Il l'exhorte à la tempérance,
　　Il fait appel à sa fidélité ;
　　　　Dans cet abus de confiance,
Pour l'honneur du nom chien quel douloureux affront !
　　Tout en mâchant, le dîneur lui répond :
« Je t'ai vu rarement faire ainsi la bégueule,
Mon bon. Mais par hasard, voyons, ne prendrais-tu

HENRY MACQUERON *(1853–1937)*

The Virtuous Dog

Two dogs, left in the house alone, had not
Much to amuse them. One thought it might be
Well to inspect the larder, with its lot
Of foods, scraps, stuffings, tidbits, temptingly
Bedecked, set out… Mused he: "Theft is a curse,
     A crime. And yet, no doubt still worse
     Is hunger. So, if one must die
By famine or the whip, what choice have I?
That food! So beautiful!… Bah! Truth to tell,
Why fret my head? Let others, by the by!"
That said, the matter weighed, the ne'er-do-well
            Delves in,
     Leaves not, thereat, a single crumb
     Untouched by his gluttonous sin…
     Whereat, in manner passing glum,
His chum, offended at his moral lack,
Urges the beast to temper his attack,
     To quit the feast lest he forget
That he casts shame on dog's fidelity,

Le fondement de ta vertu
Qu'en cette muselière emmanchée à ta gueule ?
Sur moi ton bel exemple aura peu de succès ;
Car je te dis en bon français :
Foin du serment de l'hypocrite
Qui de nécessité veut se faire un mérite. »

The honor of their race! Fangs chomping yet,
Replies the cur: "You're one to talk, my friend!
Hear my words, pray, quite clear to comprehend!
Your fine morality is counterfeit!
    That muzzle clamping tight your jaws
    Might, I fear, be its only cause!
    Alas! Fie on the hypocrite,
Who prattles, rattles on, self-righteously,
Feigning a virtue of necessity!"

HENRY MACQUERON *(1853–1937)*

Le chien et le petit chat

Alléchée par l'odeur qui monte à sa narine,
Médor en tapinois se glisse à la cuisine.
« Choisissons, se dit-il, quelque chose de bon. »
     Il ne récolte, hélas ! Que du bâton.

        Clochant, hurlant, faisant vacarme,
Pour digérer la chose il file à son chenil.
     Bon petit chat, dont l'amitié s'alarme,
Accourt le consoler. N'était-ce pas gentil ?

« Qu'ont-ils fait, ces méchants, à mon ami que j'aime ?
     Nomme-les donc, que j'aille à l'instant même…
Mais dis que tu n'as plus de mal ; ça m'en fait trop ! »
Le chien sourdement grogne et lance un coup de croc.
Petit chat jure et pleure en léchant son épaule.
Il s'en va raconter l'affaire à sa maman.
Maman Minette est bonne et promet du nanan ;
Puis dit à son amour qui doucement miaule :

« C'est la faute à ton cœur, pauvre Minet chéri,
     De trouver l'aventure étrange.
    Quand il est justement puni,
L'être sot et brutal sur l'innocent se venge. »

HENRY MACQUERON *(1853–1937)*

The Dog and the Kitten

Lured kitchenward by snout-enticing scents,
Médor, the pantry-sneak, prepares for eating.   *
"How can I choose from all this succulence,"
      He asks… He gets only a beating!

Raising a row, and now quite lame of limb,
He hobbles to his niche and, glum, will muse
Therein… A kitten-chum, shocked at the news—
      Kind soul!—attempts to comfort him.

"What did they do, the cads, to my dear friend?…
Are you in pain?… Who are they?… Heaven forfend,
I'll not forget!… They'll pay!" Whereat dog lashes
      Out with a claw and forthwith slashes
Kitten, leaves him to lick his wound, at which,
In tears, the latter quickly quits the niche…
Seeks out mammá… Weeps, wails… Minette will greet   **
      Him with an all-consoling sweet,

Saying: "It is your heart, Minet, that leads
      Your head to moan this fell event.
Best learn: when justly punished for foul deeds,
The brute wreaks vengeance on the innocent!"

---

* See p. 85, note.

** Like the dog-name Médor, the masculine Minet and the feminine Minette, with their variations Minou and Minouche, have long been common names for French cats.

HENRY MACQUERON *(1853–1937)*

Le chien et le baudet

A la porte d'une boutique,
Bazar où s'étalait un commerce exotique,
On vit, certain jour, accroupi,
Un lion à l'air débonnaire.
Vint à passer un chien dodu, luisant, bouffi,
Hormis qu'à s'admirer, instruit à ne rien faire.
Sur deux pattes il se guindait,
Au roi des animaux faisant la révérence ;
Puis il marchait avec prestance,
Quand il s'aperçut qu'un baudet
D'un œil malin le regardait.
« Connais-tu, lui dit-il, sa majesté lionne ?
Si tu savais, mon cher, quelle digne personne !
C'est un prince opulent, sage, et par-dessus tout.
Appréciateur du mérite.
De temps en temps je le visite,
Pour lui faire plaisir, car il m'aime beaucoup.
Même n'as-tu pas vu ce gracieux sourire… ?
Oui, c'est vrai, vieux jaloux. Il te va bien de rire !
Je suis bon avec toi de m'être encanaillé. »
L'âne eut bientôt du chien dégonflé la jactance,
En convainquant ce sot d'avoir fait connaissance
Avec un lion empaillé.

HENRY MACQUERON *(1853–1937)*

The Dog and the Ass

At the door of a fine emporium—
Bazaar displaying wares exotic, come
From far and wide—a lion, languid, lay
A-crouch… One day, there passed said lion's way
A dog, bright-eyed, well fed—Nay! Passing fat!—
    Who had no other skill save that
    Of finding himself fine and oh
    So fair!… He stops, stands tall, bows low
    Before the King of Beasts; whereat,
As he continues on in sprightly pace,
He notices an ass, and on his face,
A leer of mischief, whence, curiously,
He asks: "Do you not know His Majesty,
Lion? Most sage, the wisest of his race,
Most glorious Prince? My meritorious
Qualities please and flatter him. Wherefore
    I visit him and bow before
His Grace… Bah! I debase myself when thus
I speak to you! You saw him smile at me!
    And yet you snicker, sneer! Alas!
        Alack! Ah, jealousy!
        I fear your name is Ass!"
Next moment, dog stands back, rebuffed.
    His stupid pride is pricked, un-puffed—
    Deflated!—when ass proves that his
    Kingly acquaintance!—yes, he is
    A lion, to be sure… But stuffed!

FRANCIS PICABIA *(1879–1953)*

Entr'acte de cinq minutes

J'avais un ami suisse, nommé Jacques Dingue, il vivait au Pérou, à 4.000 mètres d'altitude ; parti il y a quelques années pour explorer ces régions, il avait subi là-bas le charme d'une étrange Indienne qui l'avait rendu complètement fou en se refusant à lui. Il s'était affaibli petit à petit et ne quittait même plus la cabane où il s'était installé. Un docteur péruvien, qui l'avait accompagné jusque-là, lui donnait des soins pour guérir une *démence précoce* qu'il jugeait incurable !

Une nuit, une épidémie de grippe s'abattit sur la petite tribu d'Indiens qui hospitalisait Jacques Dingue ; tous sans exception furent frappés et sur deux cents indigènes, cent soixante-dix-huit moururent en peu de jours ; très vite, le médecin péruvien affolé avait regagné Lima… Mon ami fut, lui aussi, atteint par le mal terrible, immobilisé par la fièvre.

Or, tous les Indiens morts possédaient un ou plusieurs chiens, lesquels n'eurent bientôt d'autre ressource pour vivre que de manger leurs maîtres ; ils déchiquetaient les cadavres, et l'un d'eux apporta dans la hutte de Dingue la tête de l'Indienne dont celui-ci était amoureux… Il la reconnut instantanément et sans doute en éprouva-t-il une commotion intense, car il fut subitement guéri de sa folie et de sa fièvre ; ses forces lui revinrent, alors, prenant la tête de la femme de la gueule du chien, il s'amusa à la lancer à l'autre bout de la pièce en criant à l'animal d'apporter ; trois fois le jeu recommença, le chien rapportait la tête en la

FRANCIS PICABIA *(1877–1953)*

Ahead and Behind   *

I had a friend once, a Swiss fellow, Hans Bonkers by name, He was living in Peru, twelve thousand feet up. He had gone there exploring a few years before, and had lost his heart to the charms of a strange Indian woman, who had driven him utterly out of his mind with love unrequited. Little by little he had begun to waste away until, finally, he was too weak even to leave his cabin. A Peruvian doctor who had accompanied him on his travels treated him as best he could for a *dementia præcox*, which he felt, however, to be quite incurable.

One night, a sudden influenza epidemic struck the little Indian village where Hans Bonkers was being cared for. Every one of the natives contracted the disease, without exception. In a few days, of the original two hundred, one hundred seventy-eight were dead. In a panic, the Peruvian doctor hurried back to Lima… My friend, stricken like all the rest, lay languishing with fever.

Now, it happened that all of the Indians had one or more dogs, who soon had no choice, if they were to survive, but to eat their dead masters. And so they proceeded to dismember their cadavers. One of them came trotting into Hans Bonkers' hut, carrying in its mouth the head of the Indian woman he adored… He recognized it at once. The shock, I imagine, was so intense that it jarred him back to his senses, curing him of both his fever and his madness. He took the head in his hands and, with renewed vigor, playfully threw it across the room, telling the dog

---

* My shamelessly manufactured title of this prose poem is, under the circumstances, more meaningful than that of the original, *"Entr'acte de cinq minutes"* (Five-Minute Intermission), an interlude in Picabia's surrealistic *Jésus-Christ Rastaquouère*, with which it bears no obvious relation.

tenant par le nez, mais à la troisième fois, Jacques Dingue l'ayant
lancée plus fort, elle se rompit contre le mur et, à sa grande joie,
le joueur de boule put constater que le cerveau qui en jaillit ne
présentait qu'une circonvolution et affectait à s'y méprendre la
forme d'une paire de fesses.

to "go fetch!" Once, twice, three times… And the beast would dutifully retrieve it, clutching it by the nose, in its teeth.

But the third time Hans Bonkers bowled a little too hard, and the head smashed against the wall. As the brain rolled out he was delighted to observe that it consisted of two smooth, rounded hemispheres, that looked for all the world like a pair of firm buttocks…

ABEL BONNARD *(1883–1968)*

Le vieux chien

Autrefois, enivré de ses membres robustes,
Il sautait dans la haie et griffait les arbustes,
Et ses bonds chaleureux nous fêtaient.

                              Aujourd'hui
Son âme humble est déjà recouverte de nuit.
Il somnole ; le feu lui souffle sa fumée.
Mais quand nous approchons, sa prunelle embrumée
S'ouvre, il lève vers nous sa tête avec effort,
Et cherche dans nos yeux si nous l'aimons encor.

ABEL BONNARD *(1883–1968)*

The Old Dog

Time was when he, robust of limb, would rush
Headlong against the hedge, paw, claw the brush,
Greet us with loving leaps and bounds.

                                       Today,
Humble of soul, veiled in night's black and gray,
Hearthside, he lies a-doze, as fire wafts clouds
Of smoke… But we draw near, and, through the shrouds,
He tries to raise his head. Eyes dimmed, he will
Gaze at us, wondering if we love him still.

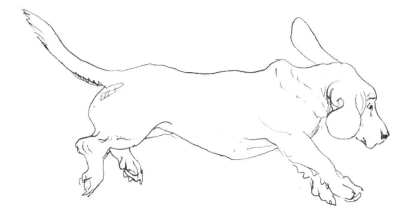

Le premier chien

C'est un chien abrupt dans sa race,
C'est le premier de tous les chiens,
Première fois que dans l'espace
Aboya ce qui n'était rien.
Il est tous les chiens à venir
Et les voudrait mener à bien,
Il est l'angoisse qui soupire
Tout en étant qu'un pauvre chien,
Il cache en lui tant de miracles
Qu'il pose un peu craintif les pattes
Sur le sol qui le porte au loin
Et si multiple qu'il en tremble,
Si fou de tout ce qu'il contient
Qu'on l'aperçoit sur une route
De plaine comme un chien courant,
Qu'on le retrouve saint-bernard
Sur le versant d'une montagne,
Près des moutons chien de berger
Et près des hommes chien de garde,
Il est toujours là qui regarde
Pour ne pas être un étranger.

JULES SUPERVIELLE *(1884–1960)*

The First Dog

He—dog abruptly, suddenly
Appearing—first dog of his race,
The first to bark at empty space,
Nothing at all to see… Yes, he
Is every dog that yet will be,
Eager to lead the pack apace
Into the future… Who sighs, pants
When pain harries his timid stance.
Poor dog… But in him there abound
Miracles as he paws the ground
That carries him far off. So many
Miracles, that, when all or any
Move him, they make him quiver, quake,
So crazed at each miraculous
Endeavor, that we take him for
A racing hound coursing the plain,
A Saint-Bernard with ski-slope chore,
A sheepdog with his flock… Or, as
Man's watchdog guard… And yet, however
He may be seen by us, he has
That knowing look! Dog: stranger never…   *

---

*The reader will notice that, while I preserve the eminent poet's regular meter, I don't presume to "correct" the non-rhymes of some of his latter lines.

PIERRE MENANTEAU *(1895–1992)*

Le vieux et son chien

S'il était le plus laid
De tous les chiens du monde,
Je l'aimerais encore
A cause de ses yeux.

Si j'étais le plus laid
De tous les vieux du monde,
L'amour luirait encore
Dans le fond de ses yeux.

Et nous serions tous deux,
Lui si laid, moi si vieux,
Un peu moins seuls au monde
A cause de ses yeux.

PIERRE MENANTEAU *(1895–1992)*

The Old Man and His Dog

Of all the ugly dogs,
Even if he might be
The ugliest, still would
I love him tenderly,
Just for his eyes.

Of all ugly old men,
Even if I might be
The ugliest, still would
Love's light shine tenderly,
Deep in his eyes.

And we would always be
Less alone. And we would—
Me, old, and ugly, he—
Share love's sweet company—
Just for his eyes.

MAURICE CARÊME *(1899–1978)*

Le petit chien

Je suis un petit chien.
Mon poil ne sert à rien
Qu'à salir les bas blancs
Que je heurte en jouant.

Je suis un petit chien
Et je ne garde rien,
Pas même un bout de miche
Dans un coin de ma niche.

Je suis un peu voleur,
Mais bien moins que le chat.
Bien mieux que lui d'ailleurs,
Je sais prendre les rats.

J'aboie longtemps sur tout,
Je pleurniche pour rien.
Je ne suis, voyez-vous,
Qu'un chien, un petit chien.

MAURICE CARÊME *(1899–1978)*

The Little Dog

I'm just a little mutt.
My coat? No purpose but
To soil white socks as I,
Playful, run smudging by.

I'm just a little mutt,
Snug in my doghouse. But
A watchdog? Not a jot!
I'd give away the lot!

I'm skilled at petty theft—
Though less than Cat, at that!
But no kitty's as deft
As me at catching Rat.

I bark, growl aimlessly.
I whimper, whine… What for?
I'm just a dog. That's me.
A little mutt—no more…

L'enfant et le chien

Un enfant seul,
Tout seul avec en main
Une belle tranche de pain.
Un enfant seul,
Avec un chien
Qui le regarde comme un dieu
Qui tiendrait dans sa main,
La clé du paradis des chiens.
Un enfant seul
Qui mord dans sa tranche de pain,
Et que le monde entier
Observe pour le voir donner
Avec simplicité,
Alors qu'il a très faim,
La moitié de son pain
Bien beurré à son chien.

MAURICE CARÊME *(1899–1978)*

The Child and the Dog

Alone, a youngster… And,
There, in his hand,
A lovely slice of bread.
Alone, a youngster… And,
Eyeing the slice,
Much coveted—
Key to a canine Paradise!—
Agog and awed
As if the child's a very god!
Alone, a youngster… And
He bites into the slice
As all can see,
Gazing agog,
That, hungry though he is,
Calm as can be,
He gives half of that slice of his
Well-buttered, to his dog.

JEAN FOLLAIN *(1903–1971)*

Le chien des écoliers

Les écoliers par jeu brisent la glace
dans un sentier
près du chemin de fer
on les a lourdement habillés
d'anciens lainages sombres
et ceinturés de cuirs fourbus
le chien qui les suit
n'a plus d'écuelle où manger tard
il est vieux
car il a leur âge.

JEAN FOLLAIN *(1903–1971)*

The Schoolboys' Dog

For fun the schoolboys chip away at ice
on a path
by the railroad tracks
they're bundled up
in heavy dark old woolens
belted around with shiny leather
the dog that's following them
has no more bowl to eat from late at night
he's old
because he's just their age.

RAYMOND QUENEAU *(1903–1976)*

Il faut faire signe au machiniste
La dame attendait l'autobus
le monsieur attendait l'autobus
passe un chien noir qui boitait
la dame regarde le chien
le monsieur regarde le chien
et pendant ce temps-là l'autobus passa

RAYMOND QUENEAU *(1903–1976)*

You've got to signal the driver…
Madame was waiting for the bus
Monsieur was waiting for the bus
a black dog passed by with a limp
Madame looks at the dog
Monsieur looks at the dog
and in the meantime the bus passed by

RAYMOND QUENEAU *(1903–1976)*

Dans l'espace

On dirait que kékchose se passe
En fait il ne se passe rien
Un autobus écrase un chien
Des badauds se délassent
Il va pleuvoir
Tiens tiens

RAYMOND QUENEAU *(1903–1976)*

In Space

You'd think something's happ'ning to us
But no nothing's happ'ning in phact
A dog's run over by a bus
Gockers stand gocking at the act   *
Rain's in the sky
My my

---

* The misspellings, not in error, are tribute to Queneau's characteristic wordplay.

[EUGÈNE] GUILLEVIC *(1907–1997)*

Fabliette du petit chien

Que lorgnait le petit chien ?
Un os qui était le sien,

Cet os que lui avait pris
Un chien tout gros de mépris.

Le ciel ne rougissait pas
D'assister à ce repas.

L'un des chiens resta petit.
L'autre garda l'appétit.

[EUGÈNE] GUILLEVIC *(1907–1997)*

The Little Pup

Little pup sat eyeing bone.
One he used to call his own.

Burly hound came swaggering up,
Snatching bone from little pup.

Sky watched hound dine on said victual;
Didn't care one whit or tittle.

Pup's still little as before;
Hound's still hungry, wants some more.

JEAN ANOUILH *(1910–1987)*

Le couple et le petit chien

Les couples d'amants
Commençant leur vie
Ont toujours envie
D'acheter un chien.
C'est un réflexe, il est charmant.
Ils le font presque tous sans en savoir la cause…
Ils pensent que cela n'est rien
Qu'un caprice.
Au lieu d'une botte de roses,
Quel cadeau plus joli imaginerait-on
A une jeune femme ?
Un jour, de son veston
L'homme tire une petite boule vivante…
On crie.
On s'attendrit.
Et désormais l'amante,
Toujours quittée pour le bureau ou la famille.
—Cela s'ennuie vite, les filles—
Aura un petit compagnon.

Les enfants des amants sont de petits caniches…
Et ils ne savent pas qu'inconsciemment ils trichent
Avec la vieille loi du couple qui se fond
Dans un autre, avant d'atteindre le fond,
Pour que l'enfant-preuve surnage,
De cet éternel amour,
Dont le naufrage,

JEAN ANOUILH *(1910–1987)*

The Couple and the Little Dog

Couples—two lovers that is—   *
Always have one wish—hers, his—
When living together: they
First must buy a dog. What for?
They don't know. Maybe no more
Than mere reflex action, you might say,
Though a charming one, no less.
And, if you asked her or him?
Just a whim!
Still, there is no lovelier gift, I guess—
Even nicer that a rose bouquet!—
For a young miss than, one day,
When monsieur presents to her,
From his coat, a living ball of fur!
Squeals and cries,
Tears in eyes…
Now, when he leaves her alone to be
At the office or with family—
Women get bored, no surprise!—
Dog stays home and keeps her company…

Lovers' offspring spawn like poodle pups,
And our pair, with too few ups—
Only downs!—will try to mend,
Child-wise, their "eternal love,"

---

* By using trochaic lines throughout, I try to suggest Anouilh's rather capriciously changing rhythms.

153

A commencé déjà avec le premier jour.
Sentant venir une séparation prochaine
Un couple se disputait.
« Que ferons-nous de la petite chienne ? »
Elle est à moi, c'est moi qui lui donne son lait
Et ses caresses ! » disait-elle.
Il rétorquait :
« Qui donc, chaque soir
Depuis qu'elle est née, la promène
Patiemment sur le trottoir ? »

Toutes les choses sont dures
A commencer et à finir.
Les couples agonisants durent
Avant de se désunir.
Le chien mourut avant la fin de l'aventure…
Ils avaient bien tort, en somme,
De se disputer pour rien :
Les plus longues amours des hommes
Ne durent qu'une vie de chien.

Save it from the wreck that Fate above
  Had, indeed, decreed to end
  Even from the very start!
Words, spats, quarrels, fights before they part…
"What should we do with the dog?" says he. **
"Mine!" insists mademoiselle. "It's me,
  Me, who give her milk, and who
  Love her, pet her!… Me, not you!"
  "Oh? And who would, patiently,
Ever since she saw the light of day,
Each night, walk her round her sidewalk loo?
  Who? Who…?" "You…?" "What's that you say…?"

Things in life begin but finish too:
  Firsts and lasts are squabble-fraught.
Bravely will the newly-loveless pair
Bear the death-throes of their dead affair.
Try to live… But finally break the knot.
And the dog? It dies before the end. ***
  Oh, how wrong for man and wife—
So to speak!—to come to blows, my friend,
All for nothing! Man's loves—even those
Longest-lasting!—last a damn dog's life:
  Little more!
    And so it goes…

** To the astute reader who would question why the masculine *chien* of line 4 has suddenly become a feminine *chienne*, I suggest that the original desired dog is really generic. Any dog, male or female, would do, its "dogness", not its gender, being the essential issue for the prototypical dog-loving lovers.

*** Deferring to the reader unconvinced by the previous note, my neuter "it" attempts to skirt the question of the dog's dubious gender.

JEAN ANOUILH *(1910–1987)*

L'enterrement

Le chien suivait l'enterrement du maître.
               Il pensait aux caresses ;
               Et il pensait aux coups.
            Les caresses étaient plus fortes…

        Dans le cortège, on s'indignait beaucoup.
On excusait la veuve—elle était comme morte.
            On pardonnait à la maîtresse
               (Elle était morte aussi).
           Mais, qu'en la présence du prêtre,
La bonne ait pu laisser vagabonder ainsi
            Ce chien au milieu du cortège !
Ah ! Ces filles vraiment ne se font nul souci.
Quelqu'un, l'ordonnateur, la famille, que sais-je ?
Aurait dû l'obliger à attacher le chien !
Elle-même, voyons ! C'est une propre à rien
Qui n'avait même pas l'excuse du chagrin.
Pourquoi la gardaient-ils ? Un ménage d'artistes…
            De véritables bohémiens.
Ce monde-là vivait d'une étrange manière…
De coup de pied en coup de pied dans le derrière,
Rejeté à la queue du cortège, le chien
        Songeait que seule la bonne était triste ;
            La bonne qui ne disait rien,
             Et à qui ne parlait personne.
Il suivit jusqu'au bout aux côtés de la bonne.
Au cimetière, tous les deux au dernier rang

JEAN ANOUILH *(1910–1987)*

The Funeral

Trotting behind the funeral procession,
                    The master's dog
Remembers both his cuff and his caress—
                    Especially the latter.

                All Monsieur's mourners march agog
                At such an untoward indiscretion.
        Madame, poor soul, is blameless in the matter,
                    Utterly prostrate with distress.
        So too the mistress of the dear deceased
                    (Laid low, half dead!) But not the maid!
                "No! She's to blame, the thoughtless jade!…"
        "Scandalous! Just imagine!" "And the priest
Is here to boot! What must he think? To let that beast
                Follow the bier?…" "What? No one thought to
                Tell her that dogs don't just run loose?…"
                        "Really, they ought to
        Teach her a thing or two!" "What's her excuse?
Surely not grief!…" "Grief? Her? A maid?…" "Odd family!
            Artistes… Bohemians, you know…"
                And so they chatter as they go.
Kicking the dog from heel to heel… Back… Back… Till he
                    Falls far behind,
                He and the wench… But, in his mind,
        He knows that she alone—silent, ignored—
        Is truly touched, she, Monsieur's one true mourner…
        As he prepares to go to his reward,

Ils écoutèrent le discours du président
De la Société des Auteurs Dramatiques.
        A la fin, las du pathétique,
        Le chien s'avança posément
        Et, pour venger un peu la bonne,
        Il pissa sur une couronne.

Maid and dog, side by side, off in a corner,
　　Listening, as the chairman of the board
Of the Société des Auteurs Dramatiques,
　　Drones endless, empty talk, talk, talk, until
Dog, fed up with their mawkishness, and in a pique—
And, to avenge the maid I guess—turns tail, and will
　　Squat on a wreath and, calmly take a leak.

CARMEN BERNOS DE GASZTOLD
(ca. 1919–1995)

Prière du chien

Seigneur
je veille !
Si je n'étais pas là,
Qui garderait leur maison ?
Qui garderait leurs moutons ?
Qui leur serait fidèle ?
Il n'y a que Vous et moi
pour comprendre
ce que c'est que la fidélité !
Ils me disent : bon chien ! brave chien !
Des mots…
Moi je prends leurs caresses
et les vieux os qu'ils me jettent,
et j'ai l'air content !
Ils croient tellement me faire plaisir !
Je prends aussi les coups de pieds
quand ils arrivent !
Tout cela n'a pas d'importance,
Moi je veille !
Seigneur,
ne permettez pas que je meure
avant que, pour eux,
tout danger soit écarté !

Ainsi soit-il !

CARMEN BERNOS DE GASZTOLD
(ca. 1919–1995)

The Dog's Prayer

Lord
I stand guard!
If I weren't here
Who would protect their house?
Who would protect their sheep?
Who would be their true, loyal friend?
No one but You and me
Can understand
What it means to be loyal, true!
They tell me: good dog! Nice dog!
Words…
And I accept their pats
And the old bones they toss me,
And I try to look pleased!
How happy they think they make me!
And I accept the kicks as well
That come my way!
But none of that matters.
I just stand guard!
Lord,
Please don't let me die
Before the dangers that they face
Are cast aside!

Amen. So be it!

RENÉ-GUY CADOU *(1920–1961)*

Des chevaux et des chiens

Les chevaux et les chiens
Parlent mieux que les hommes
Et savent de très loin
Reconnaître le ciel

Ils n'ont pour eux que l'herbe
Et la grave tendresse
Des bêtes qui remuent
Tristement le passé

Mais dans leurs yeux inquiets
Des choses et des hommes
Passe parfois l'éclair
D'une saison future.

RENÉ-GUY CADOU *(1920–1961)*

Of Horses and Dogs

The horses and the dogs
speak better than men do
and from far off are able
to recognize the sky

Nothing but grass is theirs
and mournful tenderness
of those sad creatures who
go stirring up the past

But in their restless eyes
teeming with things and men
now and then streaks the flash
of seasons yet to come.

MADELEINE REYNAUD *(contemp.)*

Le petit chien

Je suis un petit chien
Mais j'ai déjà quinze ans.
Si je présente bien,
Mon âge, je le sens.

Mon cœur est fatigué,
J'ai des douleurs partout,
Ma vue a bien baissé,
Je n'entends plus du tout.

J'aimais bien la montagne
Quand j'étais casse-cou.
Le vertige me gagne,
Je fatigue beaucoup.

Je vais plus doucement
Et je marche très peu.
Je dors bien plus longtemps,
J'ai caché tous mes jeux.

Quand une chienne passe,
Je redeviens fringant,
Je fais preuve d'audace,
Je me sens élégant.

Mais dès qu'elle est partie,
Je retrouve mon âge

MADELEINE REYNAUD *(contemp.)* *

The Little Dog

A little dog am I,
Fifteen years old! You see
How pert I am, how spry,
But my years weigh on me!

My strength is disappearing,
I ache, my heart grows tired.
My sight grows dim, my hearing
Leaves much to be desired!

I loved the hilltops' height:
Reckless my revelry,
But dizziness now, quite,
Makes a fine fool of me!

Slowly I move, and frisk
No more at all. My play?
Gone now my tricks—brash, brisk.
I sleep the day away...

But when a bitch appears,
Once more I preen and prance—

---

* I cannot vouch for the scant information available on this poet. What is definite, however, is that she should not be confused with the celebrated actress Madeleine Renaud (1900–1994), wife and frequent co-star of actor Jean-Louis Barrault.

Et mon dos s'arrondit :
Ce n'était qu'un mirage.

Mes maîtres m'aiment autant
Que quand j'étais petit.
Ils me disent souvent
Que j'ai changé leur vie.

La mienne aura été
Faite de grandes joies,
J'aurai été choyé,
J'aurai été un roi.

Quand il faudra partir,
Je ne gémirai pas.
Je voudrais m'endormir
Blotti entre leurs bras.

And itch, despite my years!—
To show my elegance.

But when she leaves, ah, then
Done is my badinage.
My back hunched once again—
She was a mere mirage!

My masters love me yet,
Though I'm no puppy now,
But I'm no less the pet
That "changed their lives" somehow.

My own will have been spent
In joyful dallying,
Coddled in love, content,
I shall have been a king.

And when time comes to die,
I'll sleep—not weep or whine—
Nestled snug, cuddled by
The arms of masters mine.

KHAMLIENNE NHOUYVANISVONG *(contemp.)*

« Vie de chien… »

Vie de chien
Le printemps pointe son nez,
Le soleil commence à chauffer
La nature, aux premiers rayons s'éveille
Tout l'hiver endormi, sommeille.
Fidèles au rendez-vous, habitude aidant,
Le chien et son maître s'installent,
A la même place que la saison précédente,
Accolé au mur, à côté du platane,
Le maître arrange son petit coin…

KHAMLIÈNE NHOUYVANISVONG *(contemp)*

"A dog's life…"

A dog's life…
Springtime points her snout.
The sun begins to spread about his heat,
Nature, with her first shining rays, awakes,
Winter, worn out, goes dozing sleepily.
Creatures of habit, master and dog—
Faithful, on schedule—settling in
Just where they did last season past,
Lean, back to wall, beside the plantain tree.
Master sets up his little corner there…

CHANTAL ABRAHAM *(contemp.)*

Mon copain

mon copain
quand j'ai du chagrin
il ne me dit rien
il sait bien
que ça ne sert à rien
quand j'ai du chagrin

mon ami
quand j'ai de la peine
il ne me dit pas qu'il m'aime
je sais bien que ça le gêne
quand j'ai de la peine

alors il m'écoute
moi je sais qu'il m'entend
et il me regarde
moi je sais qu'il comprend

il se met dans un coin
ses yeux
sont plus malheureux
que les miens

CHANTAL ABRAHAM *(contemp.)*

My Friend   My Chum

My friend   my chum
when I grow glum
he's not so dumb
best to become
silent   mum
when I grow glum

my chum   my friend
when I grow grim
doesn't profess his love   not him
just sadly stands proper and prim
when I grow grim

listens to me
stands   hears me out
looks at me
understands   no doubt

and crouching in a corner he
looks solemnly
with eyes that even sadder shine
than mine

mon copain
mon ami
il est plus qu'un ami
plus qu'un bon copain
puisque c'est mon chien

my friend   my chum
even more yet
more than a friend
more than a chum
my dog   my pet

PIERRE CORAN [*pseud.* Eugène Delaisse] *(b. 1934)*

Le lévrier et la gazelle

Dans le détroit des Dardanelles,
Au club des sports animaliers,
      Un lévrier,
      Une gazelle
Sur le stade ont sympathisé.
En vue du meeting annuel,
Le chien choisi le marathon,
La gazelle le triathlon.

L'entraînement fut rigoureux
Et grand l'espoir d'une médaille.

Au coup d'envoi et vu l'enjeu,
      Tudieu ! Morbleu !
      Double bataille.
      Preux, valeureux
      Furent tous deux.
Mais au final, vaille que vaille,
Pas de trophée ni de médaille.
Il n'empêche que leur fair-play,
En de pareilles circonstances,
Les rapprocha comme il seyait
Au-delà de leur différence.

Une amitié vaut mieux en somme
Qu'une place sur un podium.

PIERRE CORAN [*pseud.* Eugène Delaisse] *(b. 1934)*

The Greyhound and the Gazelle

Among the animals that haunt
A sports club by the Hellespont—
　　　The Dardanelles—
　　　A fleet gazelle's
Companion is a greyhound, bound
In friendship… For the yearly round,
The hound will run the marathon,
And the gazelle, the triathlon.

Zounds and gadzooks! The cries resound…
Training against each other, they
　　　Pitted their strength,
　　　Seeking the day
　　　When one would be
　　　By victory
　　　And trophy crowned…

　　　Alas! At length,
Though noble were their valiant feats,
For all their efforts, at the meet's
Conclusion: nothing! Trophy? None!
Naught but the knowledge that their very
Sportsmanly conduct exemplary—
Despite their differences—had won!

More than life's laurels, in the end,
No prize is worth more than a friend.

PIERRE CORAN [*pseud.* Eugène Delaisse] *(b. 1934)*

Les chiens et le Parlement

S'il faut en croire un reporter
Qui a le micro baladeur,
Des canidés de toutes races
Se seraient plantés, ce matin,
En rangs serrés, à la terrasse
Du Parlement européen.
Sur un podium improvisé,
Un doberman parlant français,
— Ce qui, ma foi, est peu courant—
Aurait annoncé, à tout vent :
« Chers Députés, chers Commissaires,
A l'heure où la bestialité
Est prônée par des inhumains,
Nous, les chiens, ne pouvons nous taire.
De tout temps, aux côtés des hommes,
Nous fûmes, nous restons, nous sommes,
Des gardes et des compagnons.
Depuis toujours, beaucoup le sont
Pour les enfants qui n'ont que faire
De ces conflits, de ces misères
Et de ces quartiers mis à feu.
Dans les rues, nous souffrons comme eux.
Vous en sauvez, les protégez.
Pour nous vivant à leurs côtés,
Soyez aussi un bouclier. »
Le doberman fut salué
Par des aboiements chaleureux

PIERRE CORAN [*pseud.* Eugène Delaisse] *(b. 1934)*

The Dogs and the European Parliament

A TV personality—
Mike-wielding anchor, news bloodhound!—
Announced with full authority
That canine droves were thronging round
The European Parliament
Today, of every breed, all come
To demonstrate… A podium
Appeared, where a magnificent
Doberman—one who (rather rare!)
Spoke French—harangued the crowd spread there
Before him: "*Messieurs dames,* pray heed
The message that I bring… These days,
When humans preach inhuman ways,
We dogs are wrong—oh, wrong indeed!—
If we would simply hold our tongue!
Long have we lived our life among
Their midst—companions, guides—and we
Have spent our time especially
With their young offspring, innocent
And uncorrupted, never meant
To suffer strife, war, conflagration.
Woes wrought by Man: trial, tribulation
Suffered no less by us, intent
On shielding them! Well, best we be
Shields to our own caninity!
Our time has come! Salvation for
The canine race, now, evermore!"

Et le tintement répété
De cent clochettes de collier.
Mais comme il fallait s'en douter,
Le service d'ordre averti,
Un canon à eau à l'appui,
Se serait hâté d'arroser,
Sans le moindre ménagement,
Le groupe des manifestants.
C'est là du moins ce que prétend
Le reporter aux auditeurs.
Propage-t-il une rumeur ?
Est-il bluffeur, faiseur d'histoires ?
          Allez savoir !

Our doberman is greeted with
A roar of approbation…   Kith
And kin, dogs by the score, all loudly
Barking in unison, and proudly
Tinkling their myriad collar-bells…
But, as one might suspect, the very
Bourgeois human constabulary
Bursts on the scene, promptly compels
One and all to disperse, and later,
Douses each would-be demonstrator
With water-cannon! Off they flee,
Well soaked, but no less happily,
Glad to have raised—as one might guess—
The canine moral consciousness!
Such, the reporter-hound's report.
Teller of tales? Exaggerator?
One of the tall-tale-loving sort?
Spinner of yarns spun far and wide?
            You… You decide!

PIERRE CORAN [*pseud.* Eugène Delaisse] *(b. 1934)*

Les chiens et le saint-bernard

Au Mont-Blanc, lors du C.M.C.,
Congrès Mondial des Canidés,
Un saint-bernard a adressé
Un court discours à l'assemblée :
« Chiennes et Chiens, chers Congressistes,
Chiens de traîneau et chiens de piste,
Chiens de garde, d'appartement,
Chiens de chasse, de non-voyant,
Chiens policiers, chiens de berger,
En vos races et qualités,
Ce jour, nous devons être fiers
De figurer au dictionnaire
Et en plus, de voir notre nom
Donné à deux constellations.
Ne vivez plus en chien et chat,
Moins encore en chiens de faïence.
Nom d'un chien, faites-vous confiance.
La vie de chien vous sourira. »
L'orateur fut ovationné

PIERRE CORAN [*pseud.* Eugène Delaisse] *(b. 1934)*

The Dogs and the Saint-Bernard

Convened in Mont Blanc's lofty view,
The meeting of the W.
C. C.—World Canine Congress—was
In session… First to raise his paws
To speak, a Saint-Bernard rose up,
Addressed the group, from lowly pup
To burly hound: "Dear members all—
Mesdames, messieurs—I rise to call
Attention to the great strides which
Our race has made. Each cur, each bitch,
Hunting dogs, guide dogs, lapdogs too,
Tracking dogs with unfailing scent,
Sled dogs—great huskies corpulent!—
Sheep dogs, police dogs… All of you
Must be most proud today! Yes, very
Proud of the space the dictionary
Affords us! Why, even on high,
The 'Dog Star' in the night-black sky
Bears our name! From now on, no mere,   *

* The original here makes specific reference to the two constellations, Canis Minor and Canis Major. It is in the latter that Sirius, the "dog star," shines, the brightest star in the northern sky.

Pour son ode à la liberté.
Et truffe au vent, le croc léger,
Il regagne la Vallée Blanche,
Son chalet qui sert de relais
En attendant que se déclenche,
D'un coup, la prochaine avalanche.

Banal expressions need we hear:
Fighting 'like dogs and cats'! Nor will
One stare 'like china-dogs' on guard
By logs aflame…" Our Saint-Bernard
Urges: "Stand proud! For now, no ill
Is meant by our 'dog's life'!" He was
Hailed with a shout… Loud, long applause…
Bravos, huzzahs… And up the hill,
Snout in the air, he headed back
To his chalet, to wait until
The avalanche's next attack…

PIERRE CORAN [*pseud.* Eugène Delaisse] *(b. 1934)*

Le magnat et les chiens

Financier riche et prétentieux,
Amoureux de son effigie,
Un magnat se montrait odieux
Avec ses gens de compagnie.
Le verbe haut et l'air hautain,
Il les traitait souvent de chiens
Tant il trouvait dénaturé
Ce canidé domestiqué.
Le milliardaire, en grand seigneur,
Folichonnait sur les hauteurs
Et loin des hordes de touristes,
Il skiait volontiers hors piste.
Ce qui risquait de survenir
Survint un jour de mauvais temps :
Un pan de neige coulissant
Se dépêcha d'ensevelir
Le slalomeur malavisé.
Le sort voulut qu'il fût sauvé.
Décati, flapi, racorni,
Endormi en chien de fusil,
Il fut repéré, sans retard,
Par la truffe d'un saint-bernard.

La vie, plus souvent qu'on ne pense,
Mouche le nez de l'arrogance.

PIERRE CORAN [*pseud.* Eugène Delaisse] *(b. 1934)*

The Tycoon and the Dogs

A rich tycoon, haughty of air,
In love with his own effigy,
Arrogant, vain beyond compare,
Scorned all who shared his company.
Often could he be heard to say:
"Nothing but lowly dogs are they!"
Such was the sheer contempt in which
He held the canine race!… Our rich
Financier *grand seigneur* would frolic
On the most lofty ski-slopes, where
Vile tourist-hordes would never dare
Set ski!… Until our vitriolic
Skier, one stormy day, was hit
By fell calamity. To wit,
A snow-slide, loosed by nature's whim,
Rolled down the slope and buried him.
Like hunting-hound, curled up a-doze,
He lay in frigid, rigid pose.
Whereupon Fate, ever on guard,
Deciding straightway he should be
Pulled free, dispatched a Saint-Bernard
Who, with its strong but gentle snout,
Uncovered him and dug him out…
Saved by a dog! The irony!…

Life, more than any might suppose,
Wipes arrogance's snotty nose…

GÉRARD LE GOUIC *(b. 1936)*

« Quand ma chienne me regarde… »

Quand ma chienne me regarde
ses yeux se posent en vérité
dans mon dos sur le vaisselier
ou sur la ligne des arbres
par la fenêtre ouverte.
Elle me regarde
comme à travers une porte en perles
et c'est l'au-delà qu'elle voit
et par moments qui l'inquiète.

GÉRARD LE GOUIC *(b. 1936)*

"When my dog looks at me…"

When my dog looks at me
her eyes really light
on the dresser behind my back
or on the line of trees
outside the open window.
She looks at me
as if through a pearl-lined doorway
and what she sees is the Great Beyond
and it troubles her now and then.

JEAN-PIERRE ANDREVON *(b. 1937)*

Chien-chien à sa mémère

Qu'est-ce que c'est ?
Qu'est-ce qu'on me met ?
De quoi j'ai l'air ?

Un bonnet,
Un manteau en mohair,
Des gants
A mes pattes de devant,
Des genouillères
Et des chaussons
A celles de derrière.

Non mais !
Quelle idée
Vous avez,
Vous les mémères
A chien-chien !

C'est peut-être l'hiver,
Mais je n'ai pas froid !
Je me porte bien.
J'ai mes poils à moi.
Alors s'il vous plaît,
Laissez mon derrière
A l'air !

JEAN-PIERRE ANDREVON *(b. 1937)*

Mummykins and Her Doggum-Woggums

Enough! What's all
This folderol,
This stuff you make me wear!

A cap? A vest?
Only the best,
Modish mohair!
And mittens for my forepaws… Knitted
Knee-pads and booties, neatly fitted…
Who needs them? Not
Your doggum-woggums!

                Winter?… But
Mummykins… So? It's cold as sin,
I know! So what?
I've got
The skin,
The comfy fur I got born in,
To keep me warm against the air,
Head to derriere!

Let me
Just be
A mutt—
Butt
Bare!

MARC ALYN [*pseud.* Alain-Marc Fécherolle] *(b. 1937)*

Chien d'ombre dans la nuit
A la mémoire claire de Karnak

J'entends marcher dehors. Tout est clos. Il est tard.
        Ma lampe seule veille.
Pas de vent. Nul oiseau. Qui passe dans le noir
        à pattes de soleil ?

C'est un chien d'autrefois parti pour l'au-delà
        comme on va à la chasse
et qui revient parfois vérifier s'il a
        toujours ici sa place.

En silence il m'appelle, en l'ombre il me regarde
        avec ses yeux d'Ailleurs,
puis je l'entends courir sur son aire de garde,
        j'entends battre son cœur.

Il rôde doucement pour n'éveiller personne
        du portail au vieux puits
et l'effraie le salue de son long cri qui sonne
        en l'air pur de la nuit.

Tendre ami disparu dont l'absence me blesse,
        est-ce toi ? Est-ce toi ?
Boiras-tu quelque nuit l'eau fraîche que je verse
        dans ta jarre là-bas ?

MARC ALYN [*pseud.* Alain-Marc Fécherolle] *(b. 1937)*

Shadow Dog of Night
In bright memory of Karnak

Outside, who goes? Late… Everything shut tight…
        Only my lamp, still beaming…
No breeze, no bird… Who treads this edge of night,
        on sunset-paws, gold-gleaming?

Back from life's vast Beyond, to question me,
        this dog of yesteryear—
hound on the hunt, returning, quizzically:
        "Am I still welcome here?"

Muffled his call, his shadowed gaze… A stare
        from Elsewhere eyes… And then,
I hear his pounding heart as, here and there,
        he plies his watch again,

between the old well and the gate… Lest I
        awake, soft-pawed he goes…
The screech-owl greets him with its long shrill cry,
        midst night's pianissimos…

Dear, gentle friend, whom still my heart grieves for!
        Is it you? Is it you?
Will you lap water from your bowl once more,
        as then you used to do?

Mais rien ne me répond. Le rond de la caresse
                    réintègre mes doigts.
Est-ce mon âme aussi qui tire sur sa laisse,
                    mon chien de l'au-delà ?

No answer... None... With hugs, my arms ring round
        into a clasping bond.
Is it my soul that tugs his leash? This hound
        of mine, from the Beyond?

ROBERT PAQUIN *(b. 1946)*

Retrouvé

Quand tu n'es pas là, je deviens
Un enfant trouvé ou un chien
Perdu. Le regard égaré,
Le cœur noyé, désemparé,
Je cherche et pleure en reniflant
Des yeux, une main ou un plan
De ville ou de vie approuvé,
Pour savoir où te retrouver.

ROBERT PAQUIN *(b. 1946)*

Found Again

You leave, and I live on, star-crossed—
Foundling child, stray hound, homeless, lost—
Heart tear-drowned, weak and meaningless…
My eyes gazing on emptiness,
Weeping and sniffling, I look for
A hand to guide my searching, or
A city map—life-map, ah yes!—
To find at least your last address…

JACQUES GOURVENNEC *(1955–2013)*

« Et ma femme et les roses et le chien… »

Et ma femme et les roses et le chien… Et que vogue ma peine, comme un gémissement.

Un peu de temps, faudrait un peu de temps encore, quelques nuages gris pour quelques suffisances, une petite pluie, pas trop forte quand même, à peine un peu de vent, des dames aux camélias : ça j'aimerais aussi.

Et quelques feuilles mortes, pour un dernier décor, quelques larmes de femmes, et des hommes plein cœur.

Je voudrais que des femmes, des jeunes et des belles, des femmes d'âge mûr, entre 35 et 50 ans et même des moins belles, des belles vieilles dames aussi, celles qui peuvent encor se souvenir d'avoir un jour aimé.

Et puis, si c'est trop demander, il y aura juste la mienne, ma femme Marie-Laure, qui elle je le sais, restera la plus belle, celle qui j'en suis sûr, reviendra me parler, nettoyer son chagrin, en silence, en secret.

Bien sûr dans une de ses mains, il y aura des roses, toutes blanches peut-être ou bien peut-être pas.

Ses mains tellement belles, couleur de l'ébène, avec de longs doigts.

JACQUES GOURVENNEC *(1955–2013)*

"And my wife and the roses and the dog…"

And my wife and the roses and the dog… And let my woe go sailing off, like a low, mournful whine.

A little while longer, for just a little longer, a few gray clouds before it's enough, a gentle little rain, surely not too strong, the slightest breeze, ladies with camellias… Yes, I'd like that too.

And a few dead leaves, for a final décor, some women's tears, and stout-hearted men.

I'd want only young, pretty women, but mature, between thirty-five and fifty, and even some not so pretty, and some pretty, old ladies too, ones who can still remember having loved one day.

But then, if that's too much to ask for, there will just be mine, my wife Marie-Laure, and she, I know, will be the prettiest, and I'm sure she'll come back to talk to me, to stroke away my grief, silently, in secret.

In one of her hands, no doubt there will be roses, maybe all white ones, or then again maybe not.

Her hands, so lovely, ebony-colored, with their long fingers.

Her hands, that I loved so much, that my lips would gently graze, and quick caresses that used to tease her so.

Ses mains que j'aimais tant, effleurées de mes lèvres et de caresses brèves et qui l'agaçaient tant.

Elle reviendra, je sais, un soir ou un matin ; qu'importe.

Elle reviendra me voir, avec dans sa tête les regrets de nos cœurs.

Quand tout sera fini, quand plus rien ne sera, lorsque plus rien de cette vie n'aura jamais été, qu'un simple souvenir et que de mon passé, mais aucun demain ne s'en rappellera.

Je voudrais d'autres larmes, des vraies et puis des fausses, mais des larmes quand même ; un dernier bruissement.

Un peu plus loin en marge du cortège, il y aura un chien ; Avec ses hurlements, un souffle à peine audible, un chien tout simplement que l'on ne verra pas ;

Un chagrin d'animal et qui pleure ma peine, comme un gémissement…

She'll come back, I know, some night or some morning, no matter which.

She'll come back to see me, and, in her head our hearts' regrets.

And when it's all over, when nothing more is left, when nothing more of that life will have ever been, only a simple memory, one from my past, no tomorrow will ever remember it again.

I'd want other tears, real ones or even fake, but tears all the same, and one last rustling sound.

A little farther off, beside the cortege, there will be a dog, a dog with his howls, and a panting breath you can scarcely hear, only a dog, but one you won't see.

The grief of an animal, weeping for my woe, like a low, mournful whine…

DANIEL BOY *(contemp.)*

Le vieil homme et le chien

Transparent au regard des passants trop pressés,
Un vieil homme est assis, transi et affamé,
Sous un porche à l'abri des frimas de janvier.
Il implore un sourire, une pièce de monnaie.

Passe un chien dans la rue, un chien de pedigree,
Une voiture suit, heurte le canidé.
Aussitôt extirpés de leurs logis douillets
Accourent de partout des bourgeois empressés.

« Ne le laissez pas là, amenez-le chez moi
J'ai une couverture afin qu'il n'ait pas froid ! »
Quelques instants après, l'animal est pansé,
Dorloté, réchauffé, maintes fois caressé.

Au dehors dans la rue le silence est tombé
Tout le monde est rentré, a fermé ses volets.
Sous son porche à l'abri des frimas de janvier
Le vieil homme soudain s'est mis à aboyer.

DANIEL BOY *(contemp.)*

The Old Man and the Dog

Transparent to the hurrying passers-by,
An old man cowers—hungry, cold—as, while
Sheltered beneath chill January's sky,
He begs the merest coin, a simple smile.

Suddenly, in the street, a fine dog—one
Of pedigree!—comes darting, falls, is hit
By a car, headlong. Folks on all sides run
From bourgeois comfort, rush to rescue it.

"Don't leave him there!…" "Bring him to my place! We   *
Have blankets!…" "Keep him warm!…" Without ado,
The high-born beast is gently, lovingly
Coddled, caressed, all his wounds tended to…

The street… Calm, silent… And, as by and by
Our bourgeois, shuttered in, sit in the dark,
Sheltered beneath chill January's sky,
The old man, left alone, begins to bark…

---

*I take the liberty of rendering this scene more dramatic by multiplying the voices. Also, lest the punctilious reader object that the dog, just referred to as a neuter "it" now becomes a masculine "him", I point out that bystanders (unlike poets in need of a rhyme) tend to masculinize dogs unless specifically female.

The Poets

Abraham, Chantal *(contemp.)*
The lack of precise biographical details on celebrated poet Abraham—birth date and such—is far less important than her easily recorded accomplishments. A virtual ambassador from the world of poetry to generations of French schoolchildren, she continues to enthrall them with her many well-publicized declamation-discussions of her own and others' works. Recipient of a number of impressive awards and government honors, her verse, deceptively simple and straightforward in appearance, sings her inspiration with the poetic themes of passing time, nature, and animals… Dogs prominent among them.

Alyn, Marc [pseud. Alain-Marc Fécherolle] *(b. 1937)*
Born in Reims, Alyn displayed his precocious literary talents from an early age, and has continued to do so throughout his illustrious career, punctuated by military service in Algeria. This *chevalier de la Légion d'honneur* is known for his almost worshipful adoration of the Cat, a *"félinolâtrie"* as he terms it, that has resulted in numerous poetic achievements and honors, while not precluding admiration for the Dog as well, as skillfully evidenced in these pages.

Andrevon, Jean-Pierre *(b. 1937)*
Andrevon, born in a small town in the Auvergne, is a multi-talented novelist, painter, singer, and poet, clearly with many strings to his artistic bow. Principal among them is his prominence as a science-fiction writer with some dozen works and anthologies to his credit, as well as several published under the pseudonym Alphonse Brutsche. As will be obvious from his canine self-encomium in the poem presented in these pages, he delights as well in displaying, in his various disciplines, his wit and sardonic sense of humor.

Anouilh, Jean *(1910–1987)*
Admirers of Anouilh as a major 20th-century playwright may be surprised to see that he indulged himself, as something of a pastime, in the poetic fable as well. Born near Bordeaux, he was introduced by his musician mother to the theater at age twelve. Thanks to collaboration

in the thirties with directors like Georges Pitoeff, success soon followed success. Gradually, however, seeing his witty comedies and anachronistic historical dramas like *Antigone* (1944) supplanted by Ionesco 's and Beckett's Theater of the Absurd, he died suddenly, leaving a substantial repertoire of frequently performed masterpieces.

Arnault, Antoine-Vincent *(1766–1834)*
In and out of favor according to the prevailing political winds, Parisian *haut bourgeois* Arnault was obliged during the Terror to seek frequent refuge in Belgium and England in order to escape imprisonment. Becoming a protégé of Napoléon and named to the Institut de France, he weathered the storms thanks to his prestige as playwright and poet, eventually making peace with the Bourbons and even being elected to the Académie Française. He died while writing the memoirs of his colorful career.

Baudelaire, Charles *(1821–1867)*
Surely one of France's most important modern poets, Baudelaire lived a short and chaotic life. Writing *Les Fleurs du mal* (1857) after a stay in the South Seas, sent by his bourgeois stepfather hoping to reform his social excesses, the recalcitrant Baudelaire would see his poems censored for alleged lewdness. (For a selection, see my translations, *Selected Poems from 'Les Fleurs du mal,'* University of Chicago Press, 1998. A juxtaposition of urban beauty and decay, and the work's glorification of the ghastly nature of daily life, is reflected also in his posthumous *Petits poèmes en prose.*

Bernos de Gasztold, Carmen *(1919–1995)*
Few details are known about the life of this devout poet—whose name suggests possible Polish-Lithuanian royal ancestry—other than a childhood in the environs of Bordeaux and the rest of her hermetic life spent in the Benedictine Abbaye Saint-Louis du Temple in Vauhallan, from the end of World War II to her death. It was there that she wrote religious poems largely for children, the best known of which are the *Poèmes de l'Arche,* from which the present work is taken.

Blanche, A. de *(????–????)*
See note on p. 125.

Boisard, Jean-Jacques François Marin *(1744–1833)*
One of the most prolific followers of La Fontaine, whose subjects he studiously avoided however, Boisard was born in Caen. Preferring a life of letters to a legal career, he won several local poetry competitions and, between 1773 and 1805, published a series of successful fable collections with praise from no less a luminary than Diderot. After the eventual publication of his voluminous œuvre entitled *Mille et une fables,* Boisard, disheartened by the aftermath of the Révolution, retired to a life of solitude in his native city, dying there in undeserved obscurity.

Bonaparte, Napoléon *(1769–1821)*
Readers may well be surprised to learn of Napoléon's many respectable attempts as a student poet. His authorship of the characteristically bombastic fable in these pages is well established. See *The Literary Gazette: A Weekly Journal of Literature, Science, and the Fine Arts,* August 1, 1857, p. 732, as well as Joseph-Marie Quérard's assertion in his *Les Bonaparte et leurs œuvres littéraires* (Paris, F. Daguin, 1845) in http://www.Shanaweb.net, "Le Chien, le Lapin, et le Chasseur."

Bonnard, Abel *(1883–1968)*
Born in Poitiers and educated in Marseille and Paris, after establishing an enviable reputation with over a score of works—poetry, novels, and political tracts—that won him election to the Académie Française in 1932, Bonnard. follower of anti-semite and monarchist Charles Maurras's Action Nationale, was wooed into Fascist ranks during World War II, becoming minister of education in the Vichy regime. At the Liberation, he was condemned to death *in absentia* as a collaborator, was dismissed in disgrace from the Académie, and fled to Spain. His sentence was commuted in 1960, but he chose to remain in Madrid, where he lived until his death. One may ask if his writings are also the product of fascistic leanings? Surely we would not generalize from the single gentle and humane poem presented here—a minute example of his art. But it does, at least give us a glimmer of consolation to see him capable of "art for art's sake," unblemished by political barbarism…

Boy, Daniel *(contemp.)*
The only information I can offer regarding this talented young poet is that he is—or was, until recently—a student at the Ecole Bilingue Internationale de Baillargues. in Montpelier. I continue to research his identity and further details for future editions.

Cadou, René-Guy *(1920–1951)*
Having amassed an incredibly long list of publications—long even for an author three times as long-lived as he—Cadou spent his scarcely three decades writing in a variety of genres, but poetry most of all. Writing from his childhood, and publishing his first volume at seventeen, he continued without interruption, producing from 1937 to 1950 some thirty volumes with others appearing posthumously. Born in the Breton town of Sainte-Reine de Bretagne, and suffering from ill health throughout his short life, he seemed to be trying to compensate, by quantity (and quality, no less!), for the lack of productive time he was to enjoy. When he died in the Loire Atlantique town of Louisfert, Cadou's vast array of poetic works began to attract attention and admiration, resembling in their unadorned free-verse simplicity and depth of emotion, his elder contemporary Jean Follain (see p. 209), and other "refugees" from the days of French Surrealism.

Carême, Maurice *(1899–1978)*
Prominent Belgian writer of children's poetry much admired by adults, Carême was born in the town of Wavres, where early success in his studies led him to a brief career as a schoolteacher while, at the same time, founding two literary journals. Settling in Anderlicht in 1943, he spent the rest of his productive life there, devoting himself to a variety of literary pursuits. His work, frequently honored, was often set to music by a host of fine composers, among them the likes of Florent Schmitt and Carl Orff. At his death, widely mourned, his house was turned into a museum and home of the Fondation Maurice Carême.

Coran, Pierre [pseud. Eugène Delaisse] *(b. 1934)*
Prolific poet, novelist, and respected teacher, often too categorically considered a children's author, Coran is one of Belgium's most eminent French-language men of letters. Devoted especially to the verse fable, he slyly tunes the lyre of his model La Fontaine to his own inimitable

brand of whimsical wordplay, replete with allusions to modern technology and social concern. Born in Mons, this mercurial poet has won numerous awards throughout his kaleidoscopic, ever-flourishing career. For English versions see my *Fables in a Modern Key* (2014), *Fables of Town and Country* (2018), and the forthcoming *RhymAmusings,* all published by Black Widow Press.

Couteau, Emile *(1827–1931)*

Not a professional man of letters, Paris-born jurist and government official, Couteau did not publish the first of several fable collections until he was in his seventies. No doubt influenced by his father, a literary amateur of the same name, he graciously described himself as "un nouveau venu dans le monde des lettres, qui n'a même pas l'excuse d'être un jeune." Despite some confusion as to the exact extent of his work, collection titles, etc., we can appreciate that, in addition to traditional animal fables featuring the faithful dog Médor (see p. 85). he was also specifically inspired by 20th-century technology, for good or ill, as in his charming poem included here. Couteau, fortunately, was able to make up for his late literary start by living to age of ninety-four, as much to our own benefit as to his.

Derbigny, Valéry *(mid-19th century)*

Few details are readily available concerning this author of *Contes, fables et autres poesies,* published simultaneously in 1850, in Paris (Plon Frères) and New Orleans. Its title page describes him as a "*Chevalier de la Légion d'Honneur,* membre des sociétés académiques d'Anvers, Arras, Bordeaux, Douai, Valenciennes, etc." among other honors. "Derbigny" being a not uncommon name in Louisiana, it seems safe to assume an American connection.

Deschamps, Eustache *(ca. 1346–ca. 1406)*

A native of Champagne. Deschamps gave up his legal studies to serve kings Charles V and VI, traveling extensively on official missions, possibly as far as Egypt and Syria. As a poet, rediscovered by 18th-century scholars, he was particularly adept at composing in the *formes fixes,* introduced by Machaut into French prosody in the 13th century in contrast to the amorphous verse of an earlier age.

Diouloufet, Jean-Joseph-Marius *(1771–1849)*

Diouloufet was an important precursor of the neo-Provençal renaissance, and one of the many for whom the verse fable obviously held a special attraction. If his is not a household name today, even in the households of his native Midi, he was, no less one of the foremost practitioners of the latter-day Provençal muse. Born in Eguilles, near Aix-en-Provence, his royalist leanings obliged him to abandon an ecclesiastical career and flee to Italy, where he studied the classics. Upon his return, he put his Virgilian spirit to use in a didactic, four-canto study of sericulture entitled *Leis Magnans* ("The Silkworms"). He died in the Vaucluse, leaving works in both French and Provençal. Contemporary critics, admiring his skillful La Fontainesque tone, complained that the lyrics in his collection, *Fablos, contes, epitros et outros pouesios en vers provençaux,* might have been better known had he chosen to write them in more accessible French.

Du Bellay, Joachim *(ca. 1522–1560)*

With Ronsard, one of the most outstanding and prolific poets of La Pléiade and theoretician of the group, Du Bellay was born near Angers. Along with Ronsard and fellow poets he came under the intellectual influence of Jean Dorat at the Collège de Coqueret, and wrote exquisite sonnets in the Italian tradition as well as other varied verse forms. He spent most of his remaining years as secretary to his kinsman, the Cardinal du Bellay in Rome, where his disillusionment with the court's hypocrisy and the abuses of power became a salient theme of his poetry.

Duchapt, Claude-Théophile *(1802–1858)*

Very little is known about this poet other than his dates and his legal profession. A magistrate and *conseiller* at the Appeals Court of Bruges, his birthplace, his collection of fables, published in 1850, was of sufficient quality to earn him agreeable passing mention by Sainte-Beuve in the latter's celebrated *Causeries de lundi* (vol. 5). Duchapt's subjects are seldom original, but his style is clean if undistinguished, though occasionally rising to more memorable distinction. It is known that he died in Bruges.

Fisch, Auguste *(1814–1881)*
Little more than nothing would seem to be definitely known about this poet other than his Swiss nationality, his dates (which I cannot guarantee), and the date 1878 offered by canine fable specialist Jean-Claude Hermans for the pair of poems in his anthology, *Le Chien dans les fables,* Société des Ecrivains. 2011. (See p. 13.)

Florian, Jean-Pierre Claris de *(1755–1794)*
Born an impoverished aristocrat in Languedoc, Florian, though not an imitator of La Fontaine, ranked second to him as a fabulist, during his life and beyond. In recent years, however, this skillful versifier's popularity has waned, likely owing to the often excessive sentimentalism of his scenarios and morals. But, unlike his contemporaries, we know that his *bon sens* was something of a pose, adopted to please a straitlaced protector, and that the flesh-and-blood Florian was hardly the high-principled moralist of his fables. A distant relative of Voltaire, who supported his election to the Académie Française, Florian died after a brief political imprisonment.

Follain, Jean *(1903–1971)*
Follain was born in the small Normandy town of Canisy, whose rural pre-World War II setting of his childhood plays a prominent role in his short, straightforward, and especially transparent poems. It is felt that, after the characteristically opaque and typically "French" poetry of the Surrealists, Follain's is the voice of a healthy and welcome reaction. Although he juggled two careers, those of lawyer and poet—as did many authors of previous centuries—the almost religious devotion of more modern, doctrinaire poets to "poetry and nothing but" had finally become an unrealistic aesthetic stance. The down-to-earth, free-verse form of his poetry—like the poem in these pages—attests to his freedom from affectation.

Furetière, Antoine *(1619–1688)*
Essentially a novelist whose satiric style is not without similarities to English writers like Fielding, Paris-born Furetière indulged as well in occasional poetry. A member of the Académie Française, he is best known for his dissatisfaction with the slow pace of its projected dictionary and his decision to publish his own. That endeavor resulted for

him in the recriminatory accusation of plagiarism and dismissal from the august company's ranks, a punishment that was, however, eventually rescinded.

Gellert, Christian *(1715–1769)*

A native of Saxony, Gallert learned French as a teenager at the University of Leipzig, eventually becoming a skilled poet in that language. So skilled, in fact, that his publication of fables, dating from 1748, earned him an accusation of having plagiarized La Fontaine. Not only did he vigorously defend his originality, insisting on his own inspiration, but he also counted among his champions Frederick the Great, who, after a personal meeting with him, voiced admiration for both his poetry and his character with the sly judgment that Gellert "was the most reasonable of all the German scholars.

Gill, André [pseud. Louis-Alexandre Gosset de Guînes] *(1840–1885)* and Gramont, Louis de *(1854–1912)*

The first-named of this duo of Montmartre denizens. Gill was both a noted artist-caricaturist and a much appreciated *chansonnier,* the latter talent evidenced in these pages. Born in Paris, he studied at the Académie Royale de Peinture et de Sculpture. A bohemian, he became one of the most familiar figures in several of the capital's cabarets, especially the *Lapin Agile,* baptized in his honor from the phrase "le lapin à Gill" (Gill's rabbit) on the sign painted by him, showing an agile rabbit jumping out of a cooking-pot. There he rubbed elbows with Picasso, Utrillo, Renoir, Van Gogh and others. Gill was tragically destined to lose his mind and end his days, after a stay in the asylum at Charenton, punctuated by a desperate escape and reconfinement.

After a colorful youth as a journalist, dramatist, and librettist, Gill's less celebrated co-poet and co-performer, Louis de Gramont, born in Sèvres and more fortunate than Gill—never losing his senses, that is— spent his later years in the rather more prosaic practice of the law.

Gourvennec, Jacques *(1955-2013)*

Born severely dyslexic, Gourvennec's disability, not recognized during his childhood and hence left untreated, deprived him of both normal speech and the benefits of an early education. After stints at painting and at unrewarding occupations, he settled for becoming a plumber, with, as he tells us, no friend to talk to but the radiator in his room. In 1999, mired in alcoholism and depression, it was a chance encounter with the poetry of Léo Ferré (1916–1993) that changed his life, freeing his trapped soul from the straitjacket of his confusion, and affording him, until his premature death, a lycée teaching career in thermal engineering. And, a career in poetry as well, resulting in his own volume, *Sale type!*, a collection of some twenty poems in a variety of styles, all miraculous for a dyslexic! Or, as in the prose poem in these pages, in a confusion of styles. But an intentional aesthetic confusion, not the one he felt as a desperate child, and whose meaning the dog-hero of that text's conclusion yearns symbolically to express through the barks and whimpers of its own dyslexic jumble…

Grécourt, abbé Jean-Baptiste-Joseph Willart de *(1683–1743)*
Possibly the descendent of a Scottish émigré family, Grécourt, born in Tours, though an ecclesiastic thanks to his mother's money, honored his vows more in the breach than in the observance. A social lion of dubious morals, he penned satirical and frequently licentious verse, often under protective assumed names. In more serious literary moments he was a skillful practitioner of the 18th-century verse fable, though the exact extent of his repertory is hard to determine given his cavalier attitude toward his own productivity.

Grozelier, père Nicolas *(1692–1778)*
Born in Beaune, Grozelier was a member of the Congrégation de l'Oratoire, teaching theology, philosophy, and belles-lettres in the order's schools, and doing research as well in physics. At his death, he left several works related to these fields. A respectable poet himself, he was author of at least two volumes of fables, each entitled *Fables nouvelles*, in 1760 and 1768, the former dedicated to the Duc de Bourgogne, grandson of Louis XIV, and the latter to the Dauphin, who would become Louis XVI. Without exaggerating Grozelier's talents and importance, it is at least significant that researcher, Hermans, in his *Le Chien dans les fables* (see p. 13), devotes more space to Grozelier's dog fables in his extensive collection than to the many other fabulists represented.

Guieu, J.-J. Ildephonse *(18??–18??)*
One of the more saccharine fabulists in these pages, Guieu was a schoolteacher in the Grenoble area, author of an 1867 collection entitled *Fables offertes à la jeunesse.* As the title suggests, ostensibly composed for the pedagogical edification of his own pupils, a few of his pithy poems—perhaps too generously represented in the Hermans anthology (see p. 13)—are presented here not for their stylistic or moral distinction, but as examples of the Dog pressed into strictly didactic literary service!

Guillevic [Eugène] *(1907–1997)*
Usually known simply by his last name and for his concise, objective style, Guillevic was born in the Breton town of Carnac. His spare free verse is often compared to the free-standing stone *menhirs* for which his birthplace is famous. After several decades of government economic service, he abandoned his financial career to devote himself to a second, as a poet. His first published volume did not appear until 1938, and consisted of unrhymed quatrains already typical of his minimalist hallmark. At his death, despite this late start, he could boast some forty collections as well as a Prix Goncourt for poetry.

Guilloutet, Abbé A.-L. *(????–18??)*
It is possible that this little known and only slightly documented author has been confused with others, e.g. abbé A.-L. Guichelet and abbé P. Philibert Guichelet. No matter. His (or whoever's) brief text—the only one of his to be included by Hermans (see p. 13)—remains eminently quotable and deserves its modest place in these pages.

Hugo, Victor *(1802–1885)*
Embodying virtually the entire early 19th-century aesthetic with his voluminous poetry, verse drama, and epic historical novels, Hugo is the uncontested giant of the French Romantic movement. Born in Besançon, he spent his long artistic life buffeted by the shifting political winds of the age, virtually worshiped by the public. The poem presented here, included in his late, long-projected collection "Les quatre vents de l'esprit" eventually published in 1881, is typical of Hugo's touching but not cloying sentimentality, dominated by a grudging acceptance of the inevitability and stark reality of death.

Krasicki, Prince Ignacy *(1735–1801)*

Rising through the ecclesiastical ranks, Krasicki, born in Polish Galicia, became archbishop of Gniezno and Primate of Poland in 1795. A leading Enlightenment figure, and a fluent speaker of French and Greek, he was celebrated as a playwright, translator, journalist, and encyclopedist, author of the first Polish novel, translated into French as *Les Aventures de Nicolas Doswiaczynski,* and was known as the "Prince of Poets" and "The Polish La Fontaine." His verse fables, not published in France until 1838, almost forty years after his death, frequently tend to be especially terse.

Lachambeaudie, Pierre *(1806–1872)*

Prolific fabulist and cabaret chansonnier Pierre Lachambeaudie was born in the Dordogne and spent much of his life in Paris practicing the quasi-religious social doctrine of the Saint-Simoniens. After the Revolution of 1848, he was imprisoned for his socialist activities and sentenced to be deported to the penal colony at Cayenne. Thanks to influential friends, however, his harsh sentence was commuted and he was allowed to spend a brief exile in Brussels, soon returning to Paris, where he lived until his death. His popular fables, clearly inspired by La Fontaine, were twice honored by the Académie Française.

La Fontaine, Jean de *(1621–1695)*

The most prominent fabulist since Aesop, La Fontaine's name is synonymous with the genre in both French and world literature. His repertory of twenty dozen verse fables sets forth in his personal, relaxed style, a good-natured cynicism toward humanity's foibles. Never neglecting the "rules" of classical French prosody, he manipulates them with a consummate ease and a complicit collaboration with his readers that earned for him the nickname "le bonhomme Jean," a hallmark that other fabulists could not duplicate. (For English translations see my volume in *The Complete Fables of Jean de La Fontaine,* University of Illinois Press, 2007.) To the Church's chagrin, La Fontaine also penned medieval-style verse *contes,* scabrous for their time, that led to a temporary excommunication. (For a selection, see my *La Fontaine's Bawdy: Of Libertines, Louts, and Lechers,* Princeton University Press, 1992, rpt. Black Widow Press, 2009.)

Le Gouic, Gérard *(b. 1936)*

A modern poet, novelist, and short story writer, Le Gouic was born in Brittany of deep-rooted peasant stock and studied at the Collège Lavoisier in Paris, where one of his influential teachers was prolific, well-respected poet Maurice Fombeure. Almost as productive, he himself was author of some three-dozen volumes of poetry from 1958 to 2015, several receiving a variety of awards. From 1958, after military service in Algeria, he remained and conducted business in Africa for ten years, but without ever giving up ties to his native Brittany. Though Le Gouic is represented in these pages by a single transparent poem, that one brief free-verse example sounds both a vague echo of his other-worldly Breton *mystique* and a touching awareness of its dog-hero's sensitivity.

Macqueron, Henry *(1853–1937)*

The three poems translated in these pages are typical of Macqueron's sprightly style and engaging morals. The title-page of his collection *Fables,* published in Paris in 1888, and containing also a letter to poet-dramatist duc Henri de Bornier (1825–1901), indicates that he was a professor of mathematics. One can be pleased that his pedagogical duties did not weigh too heavily and prevent his indulging quite successfully in his poetic avocation.

Marie de France *(ca. 1160-ca. 1210)*

First identifiable woman writer in French, Marie, ironically, seems to have spent most of her life outside the then limited confines of France, probably at the Plantagenet courts of Henri II and Richard the Lionheart. The few solid details we have are culled from her writings. She is best known for her *lais*—short verse tales of Arthurian inspiration—and her fables, the first of a genre that was to thrive throughout the course of French letters. Several of Marie's fables present dogs among their characters.

Menanteau, Pierre *(1895–1992)*

Unusually long-lived, Menanteau, born in the Vendée, outlived most of his celebrated poet-friends, among them Max Jacob, Tristan Klingsor, and Maurice Carême (see p. 206). A primary-school teacher, he eventually rose in government service to the rank of "Inspecteur d'Académie." As an author he wrote a number of stories and poems largely inspired by the geography of his birthplace. Trying his hand at literary criticism as well, he paid editorial tribute to poet Louisa Paulin in 1955 with a collection of her poems in French and (Neo-Provençal) Occitan.

Nhouyvanisvong, Khamliène *(contemp.)*
Prominent intellectual member of the Paris Laotian community, one of many countrymen sharing his common family name, Nhouyvani-svong is attached to the UNESCO mission in the capital. A diplomat and talented multilingual writer, he prefers to use French for his frequent poetic endeavors. The straightforward yet picturesque free-verse scenario included here is one of three appearing (without a date) in the *Journal Sieng Samphanh*, publication of the Union des Lao en France.

Paquin, Robert *(b. 1946)*
Prominent Canadian man of letters with several neatly fitting hats, Paquin is skilled as a poet, translator, critic, and, more recently as a film adapter, boasting numerous honors in all of them. A native of Pointe-Saint-Charles, Québec, he holds degrees from the Université de Mon-tréal and the University of London. Currently living in Montréal, he has assumed yet another hat, that of cabaret performer under the name "Docteur Bobus," juggling all his diverse abilities with success and pleasure for both himself and his public.

Perrault, Charles *(1628–1703)*
If La Fontaine's name is synonymous with the verse fable, his contemporary Perrault's is no less so with the fairy tale, a 17th-century genre that was to develop a robust international literary career. This is ironic since Perrault surely expected his heritage to rest on his more ponderous intellectual contributions. One can understand why, as godfather of the "Querelle des Anciens et des Modernes," as member of the Académie Française and of the Académie des Inscriptions et Belles-Lettres, and as author of published verse ranging in inspiration from burlesque works to religious epics, Perrault might willingly attribute authorship of his tales, in whole or in part, to his son, Charles Perrault d'Arman-cour. (Regarding this controversy, see my volume *The Fabulists French, Verse Fables of Nine Centuries,* University of Illinois Press, 1992, pp. 56–57.) It was not until 1699 that Perrault the father, translating the hundred Latin fables of Italian poet Gabriele Faerno, would be considered,

himself, an authentic fabulist. The poem presented here is from that collection.

Picabia, Francis Martinez *(1879–1953)*
A free-spirited, abstract painter and brilliant colorist, who experimented in virtually all the artistic "isms" of his period—Pointillism, Impressionism, Fauvism, Cubism—before yielding, throughout most of his career to the call of Dadaism, which he practiced in both France and the United States, Picabia was the son of an American mother and a Cuban father. A Parisian by birth, he studied at the Ecole des Arts Décoratifs, but clearly was never willing to espouse a single artistic school or philosophy, intent on changing styles "like his shirt." In his later years, no less prominent as a poet, he devoted himself to surrealistic free verse and the prose poem. Readers, though possibly objecting to my shamelessly "manufactured" title for the latter translated here, will, I think, find it at least more meaningful in context than Picabia's original: "Entr'acte de cinq minutes" (Five-Minute Interlude), which, embedded in the arrogant paean to freedom *Jésus-Christ rastaquouère*, bears, as one might expect, no obvious relation to the perplexities of its surrounding text.

Queneau, Raymond *(1903–1976)*
Co-founder and editor of the good-naturedly Surrealist OULIPO— the OUvroir de LIttérature POtentielle—known for his wit and absurdist humor in all matters literary and linguistic—Queneau, born in Le Havre, was one of the most important modern French novelists, poets, and critics. Briefly a reporter for the right-wing paper *L'Intransigeant* (after its far-left beginnings) and, during World War II, in charge of the literary history division of Gallimard's prestigious *Encyclopédie de La Pléiade,* he flirted for a time with the Surrealists under Breton (to whom he was related by marriage), finally renouncing them and their Communist affiliations. Returning from military service and throughout his prolific creative career, his poetry—like the mathematically conceived *tour de force* of his hundred thousand billion (!) potentially creatable and re-creatable sonnets, as well as his prose—like the no-less math-inspired *Exercices de style,* and the colloquially challenging *Zazie dans le metro,* all displayed his hallmark of a cynical, almost playful originality.

Reynaud, Madeleine *(contemp.)*

Few French female names seem to invite an easier identification than the common "Madeleine Reynaud." Unfortunately. The surname's various possible spellings compound the difficulty, as do its several well-known, little-known, and even unknown possessors. Regrettably, I cannot offer any solid information on this poet, whose touching eulogy to her dog appears to have come from a contemporary blog. Not even her birth-date. What is definite, however, is that she should not be confused with the celebrated actress Madeleine Renaud (1900–1994), wife and frequent co-star of famous actor Jean-Louis Barrault.

Rollinat, Maurice *(1846–1903)*

A diabolical-looking poet and musician, Rollinat, a native of Châteauroux, eventually joined the Parisian avant-garde, boasting a literary and aesthetic kinship with Baudelaire, unabashedly depicting the horrors of physical degradation and death. Some critics went so far as to consider him even more sincere than his model in the "depth of his diabolism." Rollinat himself set many of his over one hundred poems to music, and would frequently perform them with other-worldly brio at the famed Montmartre cabaret "Le Chat Noir." Losing his mind after the death of his wife from rabies, he died tragically in an asylum.

Segrais, Adeline Joliveau de *(1756–1830)*

Born to a well-to-do family in Bar-sur-Aube as Marie-Madeleine-Nicole-Alexandrine Gehier, Joliveau de Segrais spent most of her life in Paris, preferring—thanks to her considerable erudition and fluency in several languages—to home-school her five children rather than entrust them to the educational ravages brought on by the Révolution. To this end, and encouraged by various colleagues, she published three editions of her original fables (and other poems) between 1801 and 1814, in which animal characters—dogs among them—typically predominate.

Ségur, Anatole Henri de *(1823–1902)*

Second of the eight children of the eminent Sophie Rostopchine, comtesse de Ségur— daughter of the governor-general of Moscow who saved it from the Napoleonic advance in 1812, and herself the author of two dozen wildly successful little moral tales—Ségur, on his father's side, was great-grandson of a general who had fought in the American Revolution under Rochambeau and was ambassador to the court of Catherine the Great. *Chevalier* and *officier de la Légion d'honneur,* not surprisingly, Ségur's many political writings show his staunch allegiance to Throne and Altar, just as his several disparate volumes of *Fables,* beginning with a collection in 1847 and punctuating his career, generally reflect traditional moral values in an attempted La Fontaine style. Their frequent pomposity and "preachiness" is often relieved, as here, by welcome flashes of humor.

Stassart, Goswin-Joseph-Augustin baron de *(1780–1854)*
A Belgian-Dutch politician, Stassart spent most of his career embroiled in the political machinations of his newly-forming country, studying economics in Paris and fulfilling a number of important governmental functions, while at the same time attempting to win his colleagues over to his deeply held devotion to freemasonry. As a writer he served as president of the Académie Royale de Belgique, gaining an impressive reputation for his fables and various other writings—a reputation that has not stood the test of time, despite a clear, straightforward, but uninspired style and morals of sound but conventional *bon sens.*

Supervielle, Jules *(1884–1960)*
A leading poet and prose writer of the 20th century, Supervielle, born in Montevideo, divided his time between that city and Paris. Beginning to write at age nine, his early poetry won praise from André Gide and Paul Valéry, and, like St. Jean Perse, a fellow tropical French-language poet, he was admired—adulated—by none other than T. S. Eliot, who predicted for both an unquestionable literary immortality. Nominated several times for the Nobel Prize, and *officier de la Légion d'honneur,* five years after his election to the Académie Française and his receipt of the Grand Prix de Littérature, this poet of time and space, of exile and separation, of the timelessness of the soul, died in Paris, his spiritual home.

Tardy, Marc-Louis de *(1769–1857)*
Staunch royalist, Tardy, born in Montluçon, survived the Révolution by emigrating until the return of the Bourbons, who named him *chevalier de la Légion d'honneur* in 1814. With Napoléon's escape from Elba, Tardy, during the Cent Jours, actively opposed the Emperor's continu-

ing ambitions. His support for Louis XVIII earned him a *marquisat,* and led to his election to a variety of government posts over the next two-plus decades. With the death of his wife, he devoted himself to a youthful love of literature, publishing his *Fables et tragédies* in 1839, containing two early plays, *Cromwel* [sic] and *Synna,* as well as a dozen fables, at least some of which may also have dated from his youth, and most of which, using typical animal characters, albeit not without skill, veiled his social and political views.

Vitallis, Antoine *(1749–1830)*
The only biographical or other documentation for Vitallis—a shadowy Parisian, it would seem—can be found in the authoritative Hermans anthology (see. p. 13). We are told there that the poet composed a collection consisting of four books of twenty-six fables, though with no indication of title or date, and are assured that he was married and "a good father." That positive judgment appears to be confirmed by the single poem of his that I have been able to locate, the one translated in these pages.

NORMAN R. SHAPIRO, honored as one of the leading contemporary translators of French, holds the B.A., M.A., and Ph.D. from Harvard University and, as Fulbright scholar, the *Diplôme de Langue et Lettres Françaises* from the Université d'Aix-Marseille. He is Professor of Romance Languages and Literatures, Distinguished Professor of Literary Translation, and Poet-in-Residence at Wesleyan University and is currently Theater Adviser at Adams House, Harvard University. His many published volumes span the centuries, medieval to modern, and the genres: poetry, novel, and theater. Among them are *Four Farces by Georges Feydeau; The Comedy of Eros: Medieval French Guides to the Art of Love; Selected Poems from Baudelaire's 'Les Fleurs du Mal'; One Hundred and One Poems of Paul Verlaine* (recipient of the Modern Language Association's Scaglione Award); *Negritude: Black Poetry from Africa and the Caribbean;* and *Creole Echoes: The Francophone Poetry of Nineteenth-Century Louisiana.*

A specialist in French fable literature, Shapiro has also published *Fables from Old French: Aesop's Beasts and Bumpkins* and *The Fabulists French: Verse Fables of Nine Centuries.* His translations of La Fontaine are considered by many to be the definitive voicing into English of this famed French poet. His critically acclaimed volumes include *Fifty Fables of La Fontaine; Fifty More Fables of La Fontaine; Once Again, La Fontaine;* and *The Complete Fables of Jean de La Fontaine,* for which he was awarded the MLA's prestigious Lewis Galantiere Prize. His monumental collection *French Women Poets of Nine Centuries: The Distaff and the Pen* won the 2009 National Translation Award from the American Literary Translators Association, as well as two awards from the Association of American Publishers in 2008.

Other titles include *La Fontaine's Bawdy: Of Libertines, Louts, and Lechers; To Speak, to Tell You? Poems by Sabine Sicaud;* and *Préversities: A Jacques Prévert Sampler.* Shapiro is a member of the Academy of American Poets, and has been named Officier de l'Ordre des Arts et des Lettres de la République Française.

OLGA K. PASTUCHIV is a children's book author, painter, and commercial illustrator of everything from murals, parade floats, and theater backdrops to printed materials such as a postcard for the St. Nicholas Anapafsas Monastery in Greece. She has illustrated a cookbook, *Culinary Potions* by Eve Berman; the award-winning children's book *Riparia's River* by Michael J. Caduto (Tilbury House); and several botany and poetry collections including *Cricket Weather* by Anthony Walton (Blackberry Press), *Crossing To Aranmor* and *Find A Place* by Glenn Shea (Vortex Press) in addition to the poster for his reading at Shakespeare & Co. in Paris. Most recently, she illustrated *Fables in a Modern Key* and *Fables of Town & Country*, Pierre Coran's two collections translated by Norman R. Shapiro (Black Widow Press), as well as Shapiro's *Fe-Lines: French Cat Poems Through the Ages* (University of Illinois Press).

Pastuchiv's picture book *Minas and the Fish* (Houghton Mifflin) is about a fisherman's boy she met on Karpathos Island while working on a fishing boat there.

She has taught woodcut on both grade-school and college levels, and exhibited in galleries in several states and countries. She currently lives in Maine.

TITLES FROM BLACK WIDOW PRESS
TRANSLATION SERIES

A Flea the Size of Paris: The Old French "fatras" and "fatrasies" **(forthcoming)**
Translated by Ted Byrne and Donato Mancini

A Life of Poems, Poems of a Life by Anna de Noailles. Edited and translated by Norman R. Shapiro. Introduction by Catherine Perry.

Approximate Man and Other Writings by Tristan Tzara. Translated and edited by Mary Ann Caws.

Art Poétique by Guillevic.
Translated by Maureen Smith.

The Big Game by Benjamin Péret.
Translated with an introduction by Marilyn Kallet.

Boris Vian Invents Boris Vian: A Boris Vian Reader.
Edited and translated by Julia Older.

Capital of Pain by Paul Eluard. Translated by Mary Ann Caws, Patricia Terry, and Nancy Kline.

Cats Great and Small: Cats All. Translated by Norman R. Shapiro; illustrated by Olga K. Pastuchiv **(forthcoming)**

Chanson Dada: Selected Poems by Tristan Tzara. Translated with an introduction and essay by Lee Harwood.

Earthlight (Clair de Terre) by André Breton. Translated by Bill Zavatsky and Zack Rogow.

Essential Poems and Prose of Jules Laforgue.
Translated and edited by Patricia Terry.

Essential Poems and Writings of Joyce Mansour: A Bilingual Anthology. Translated with an introduction by Serge Gavronsky.

Essential Poems and Writings of Robert Desnos: A Bilingual Anthology. Edited with an introduction and essay by Mary Ann Caws.

EyeSeas (Les Ziaux) by Raymond Queneau. Translated with an introduction by Daniela Hurezanu and Stephen Kessler.

Fables in a Modern Key by Pierre Coran. Translated by Norman R. Shapiro. Full-color illustrations by Olga Pastuchiv.

Fables of Town & Country by Pierre Coran. Translated by Norman R. Shapiro. Full-color illustrations by Olga Pastuchiv.

Forbidden Pleasures: New Selected Poems 1924–1949 by Luis Cernuda. Translated by Stephen Kessler.

Furor and Mystery & Other Writings by René Char. Translated by Mary Ann Caws and Nancy Kline.

The Gentle Genius of Cécile Périn: Selected Poems (1906–1956). Edited and translated by Norman R. Shapiro.

Guarding the Air: Selected Poems of Gunnar Harding. Translated and edited by Roger Greenwald.

Howls & Growls: French Poems to Bark By. Translated by Norman R. Shapiro; illustrated by Olga K. Pastuchiv.

I Have Invented Nothing: Selected Poems by Jean-Pierre Rosnay. Translated by J. Kates.

In Praise of Sleep: Selected Poems of Lucian Blaga Translated with an introduction by Andrei Codrescu.

The Inventor of Love & Other Writings by Gherasim Luca. Translated by Julian & Laura Semilian. Introduction by Andrei Codrescu. Essay by Petre Răileanu.

Jules Supervielle: Selected Prose and Poetry. Translated by Nancy Kline & Patricia Terry.

La Fontaine's Bawdy by Jean de La Fontaine. Translated with an introduction by Norman R. Shapiro.

Last Love Poems of Paul Eluard. Translated with an introduction by Marilyn Kallet.

Love, Poetry (L'amour la poésie) by Paul Eluard. Translated with an essay by Stuart Kendall.

Pierre Reverdy: Poems, Early to Late. Translated by Mary Ann Caws and Patricia Terry.

Poems of André Breton: A Bilingual Anthology. Translated with essays by Jean-Pierre Cauvin and Mary Ann Caws.

Poems of A. O. Barnabooth by Valery Larbaud. Translated by Ron Padgett and Bill Zavatsky.

Poems of Consummation by Vicente Aleixandre. Translated by Stephen Kessler.

Préversities: A Jacques Prévert Sampler. Translated and edited by Norman R. Shapiro.

The Sea and Other Poems by Guillevic. Translated by Patricia Terry. Introduction by Monique Chefdor.

Through Naked Branches by Tarjei Vesaas. Translated, edited, and introduced by Roger Greenwald.

To Speak, to Tell You? Poems by Sabine Sicaud. Translated by Norman R. Shapiro. Introduction and notes by Odile Ayral-Clause.

MODERN POETRY SERIES

BARNSTONE, WILLIS.
ABC of Translation
African Bestiary **(forthcoming)**

BRINKS, DAVE.
The Caveat Onus
The Secret Brain: Selected Poems 1995–2012

CESEREANU, RUXANDRA.
Crusader-Woman. Translated by Adam J. Sorkin.
    Introduction by Andrei Codrescu.
Forgiven Submarine by Ruxandra Cesereanu
    and Andrei Codrescu.

ESHLEMAN, CLAYTON.
An Alchemist with One Eye on Fire
Anticline
Archaic Design
Clayton Eshleman/The Essential Poetry: 1960–2015
Grindstone of Rapport: A Clayton Eshleman Reader
Penetralia
Pollen Aria
The Price of Experience
Endure: Poems by Bei Dao. Translated by
    Clayton Eshleman and Lucas Klein.
Curdled Skulls: Poems of Bernard Bador. Translated
    by Bernard Bador with Clayton Eshleman.

JORIS, PIERRE.
Barzakh (Poems 2000–2012)
Exile Is My Trade: A Habib Tengour Reader

KALLET, MARILYN.
How Our Bodies Learned
The Love That Moves Me
Packing Light: New and Selected Poems
Disenchanted City (La ville désenchantée)
    by Chantal Bizzini. Translated by J. Bradford
    Anderson, Darren Jackson, and Marilyn Kallet.

KELLY, ROBERT.
Fire Exit
The Hexagon

KESSLER, STEPHEN.
Garage Elegies

LAVENDER, BILL.
Memory Wing

LEVINSON, HELLER.
from stone this running
LinguaQuake
Tenebraed
Un-
Wrack Lariat

OLSON, JOHN.
Backscatter: New and Selected Poems
Dada Budapest
Larynx Galaxy

OSUNDARE, NIYI.
City Without People: The Katrina Poems

ROBERTSON, MEBANE.
An American Unconscious
Signal from Draco: New and Selected Poems

ROTHENBERG, JEROME.
Concealments and Caprichos
Eye of Witness: A Jerome Rothenberg Reader.
    Edited with commentaries by Heriberto Yepez
    & Jerome Rothenberg.
The President of Desolation & Other Poems

SAÏD, AMINA.
The Present Tense of the World: Poems 2000–2009.
    Translated with an introduction by
    Marilyn Hacker.

SHIVANI, ANIS.
Soraya (Sonnets)

WARD, JERRY W., JR.
Fractal Song

ANTHOLOGIES / BIOGRAPHIES

*Barbaric Vast & Wild: A Gathering of Outside and
Subterranean Poetry (Poems for the Millennium,
vol. 5).* Editors: Jerome Rothenberg and
John Bloomberg-Rissman

Clayton Eshleman: The Whole Art by Stuart Kendall

Revolution of the Mind: The Life of André Breton
by Mark Polizzotti

WWW.BLACKWIDOWPRESS.COM